LEADING
FROM
HORSEBACK

JIM COWART

LEADING

FROM

HORSEBACK

Lost Lessons Every Church Leader Needs

Abingdon Press™
Nashville

LEADING FROM HORSEBACK:
LOST LESSONS EVERY CHURCH LEADER NEEDS

Copyright © 2018 by Abingdon Press

Library of Congress Cataloging-in-Publication Data has been requested.

ISBN 978-1-5018-0338-3

Scripture quotations noted CEB are taken from the Common English Bible, copyright 2011. Used by permission. All rights reserved.

Scripture quotations noted KJV are from The Authorized (King James) Version. Rights in the Authorized Version in the United Kingdom are vested in the Crown. Reproduced by permission of the Crown's patentee, Cambridge University Press.

Scripture quotations noted NKJV are from the New King James Version®. Copyright © 1982 by Thomas Nelson. Used by permission. All rights reserved.

Scripture quotations noted NLT are taken from the Holy Bible, New Living Translation, copyright © 1996, 2004, 2015 by Tyndale House Foundation. Used by permission of Tyndale House Publishers, Inc., Carol Stream, Illinois 60188. All rights reserved.

Photographs by Skye Mills are reproduced by permission from Jim Cowart. All rights reserved.

18 19 20 21 22 23 24 25 26 27—10 9 8 7 6 5 4 3 2 1
MANUFACTURED IN THE UNITED STATES OF AMERICA

**Dedicated to some of my unsung heroes—
the Circuit Riders**

Special Thanks:

*To my daughter, Aly Cowart, for help with discussion questions
To Skye Mills, for the photos
To Ginger Anderson with Sun Valley Arabians, for Seri's hair and makeup
To Jen Cowart for her support
To Harvest Church—I love you guys!*

CONTENTS

CONTENTS

INTRODUCTION

T his book is about leadership. You might be wondering what a leadership book has to do with horses and vice versa. It's a good question. This book contains the lessons I've learned from horses about guiding and growing a church. My wife, Jen, and I started Harvest Church near Macon, Georgia, in 2001 with four people. Since then, Harvest Church has grown with more than two thousand people in weekly attendance.

Think of this book as a collection of lessons in cross-training, which is what happens when we apply skills from one discipline to a completely different field. A good example of cross-training is the three-hundred-pound offensive lineman who takes ballet lessons to improve his flexibility and quickness on the football field. He'll probably feel a little awkward at first. He'll probably never dance *Swan Lake* professionally, but when his improved flexibility skills help him beat his opponent off the line, it's been worthwhile. The cross-training goal of this book is to take lessons from horseback and apply them in the leadership arena. These training lessons from the equine world aren't new or secret. But they may be forgotten or overlooked by the average person in our modern world who doesn't have much contact with horses.

The age of the horse has passed. The era when the horse was the cutting-edge technology for transportation, agriculture, and war is long gone. Once called "king maker" because civilizations rose and fell under the hoofbeats, the horse has now become relegated to entertainment and recreation.

While horses aren't extinct or endangered as a species, and can still be seen just outside of urban areas grazing in pastures, few people have actually had the experience of riding a horse, even on vacation or at a county fair. But even fewer people have a long term relationship with horses today. "Horse people" ride them, care for them, and learn to speak their silent language. The "people of the horse," such as our Native Americans and the bedouins of the Middle East, didn't merely keep horses. They lived with them in their tents. They shared their food and water. They formed a bond of respect, admiration, and partnership. There was celebration in the community when a filly was born! Horses meant wealth and speed, power and freedom. Subtle lessons gleaned from living with horses have now been mostly lost or forgotten.

So, saddle up! It doesn't matter whether you're a "horse person" or not. You're about to discover some helpful insights about leadership from our noble friend the horse that will help you be a better leader in your church, home, and business.

MEET THE CAST OF
CHARACTERS

The Man

Hi, my name is James Arch Cowart, Jr, but
you can call me Jim. I'm husband to Jen and
dad to Aly and Josh. I'm also the founding,
lead pastor of Harvest Church.

The Horse

Heeyyiiieeeey, I'm Serenity al Janat, but you
can call me Seri. I'm a direct descendent of an Egyptian Arabian mare
from the classic Dahmah-Shahwan
strain. I can trace my lineage back to
King Solomon's stables in Israel, but
now I live in middle Georgia with
my best buddy Jim. *Shalom*, y'all!

The Church

Hey, I'm Harvest Church—A
United Methodist Congregation, but you can call me Harvest.

I launched in 2001 and have grown as a congregation to number more than two thousand people.
I've even been named one of *Outreach
Magazine's* fastest-growing churches in
the country for several years.

CHURCHES AND HORSES NEED A LEADER

*Do you know the hardest thing about learning how to ride a horse?
The ground.*

—Old Cowboy Proverb

*[Jesus] gave some apostles, some prophets, some evangelists, and some
pastors and teachers. His purpose was to equip God's people for the
work of serving and building up the body of Christ.*

—Ephesians 4:11-12a (CEB)

Nobody Likes "Horsey" ...
Not Even Horses

I'd been out of town, overwhelmed, out of sorts, and stressed
out. It had been about two weeks since I'd seen and ridden
Seri, my sweet Arabian mare. I hugged her neck as she came
to greet me, and I was sure she was as glad to see me as I was to
see her. I grinned as she loaded on the trailer, anticipating the
freedom and partnership I was about to encounter with my horse

1

friend on the trails. I could see it already—running through the forest paths, wind blowing in our hair, sunshine beaming down. All would be right with the world again.

I expected too much.

Things went well at first. The day was nice. The sun was shining. But my daydream of a joyful reunion with my horse was not working out. There was something very important that I had forgotten: Seri is horse, not a person. That means she thinks like a horse and acts like a horse. And as much as I love her and want her to be Trigger (Roy Rogers's horse) or Silver (the Lone Ranger's horse) I try to remember that's Hollywood and this is real life. And this day Seri was acting rather "horsey."

If you're not a horse person, let me explain horsey. You probably know the difference between "childlike" and "childish." Childlike is a description for the best characteristics of children, such as trust, love, and belief. But childish describes the worst traits of children, such as selfishness, impatience, and bratiness. Well, Seri was acting horsey, like an eight-hundred-pound brat. She was fighting me with the bit in her mouth, tossing her head, and pinning her ears back in frustration and anger. My sweet horse who I love so much and dreamed about riding was being downright disrespectful. At first this hurt my feelings. Then I remembered that Seri is a horse, and I needed to start thinking like a horse too.

Horses are herd animals. They live and travel in groups, and there is a definite pecking order in their horse society. If you watch a group of horses in a pasture, it doesn't take long to discover that there is a top horse who rules the field. Horse fights happen, but usually don't last long. A nip here and a kick there by the dominant mare is enough to keep everyone in line. In fact, a simple pinning of the ears is often the only signal needed for the other horses to move out of the way and straighten up.

Horses are accustomed to leaders. They want a leader. They expect a leader. The way a person becomes a leader of horses is to make the horse move his or her feet. Behave like the dominant mare in the pasture. She asserts and establishes her position by making the other horses move. She applies subtle pressure like pinning her ears. If that doesn't work, she increases the pressure with a nip or a kick until she gets the other horse to move away from her. Lead horses in wild herds have even been known to discipline young horses who are being unruly with the horse equivalent of a "time out." They drive the troublemaker out of the herd until he is repentant and changes his behavior. When he starts acting like a respectable citizen again, he's allowed back in.

Seri's horsey disrespect toward me was in part caused by my absence. I had been gone for two weeks. Seri hadn't been ridden. She had been in the stall and pasture for two weeks, and now that I was on her back, she began to question me. Now, this is important because leaders are often asked questions that aren't put into words but acted out in behavior. People are going to question your leadership, and they often use their behavior instead of their words to ask the questions.

In Seri's horsey behavior, she was actually asking me these questions:

I haven't seen you in a while. Are you still the leader of my herd?

What makes you think you're worthy to be my leader?

Maybe I'll be the leader of our herd now. What do you think about that?

When I realized what was going on, I told her, "Listen to me, Seri. I'm glad to see you, but you better get this in your head pretty quickly. I'm the leader of this herd of two. You are invited to be my friend and my partner, but I am the leader."

Of course, words weren't enough to convey this message, so I translated this into the language she speaks, the silent language of the horse. I moved her feet. A lot. Just like a dominant mare would do. I dismounted and put her on a lunge line (a long rope) and worked her in large circles until she began to get the message. It didn't take long, and she began to ask me other silent questions. She began to lick her lips and turn her ear toward me.

Everything is training.

In doing this, she was saying in horse language, "Okay, okay. You are a good leader. Can we be friends now? I'm ready to listen to you and follow your leadership."

As soon as I removed the pressure of making her move, she came right up to me for some loving and snuggling. From here I was able to remount and continue our ride. This time was much closer to my ideal image because Seri was happy, respectful, and listening to me.

Horses need a leader. And if you as the owner or rider don't recognize this need and take the leadership position, then the horse pretty much says, "Well, if you aren't going to be the leader, I guess I'll have to take charge." By the way, if you've ever been on the back of a runaway horse you know how terrifying it can be for your horse to be the leader instead of you.

This behavior is not unique to horses. I'm sure you've met dogs that are pampered and spoiled brats. In the absence of a human leader of the pack, the dog assumes the role. It's even more tragic with children who are pampered to the point of being spoiled. Perhaps well-meaning parents abdicate their role as leader, and a little tyrant arises to rule the roost. This same pattern can happen in churches, businesses, and government too. When leadership is not clear, chaos follows.

Horses need a leader. So do children. And so do churches.

Stay in Your Lane

Here are two things I've learned about leadership:

1. Everyone can and should be a leader.
2. You've got to stay in your lane.

Some might disagree and make the case that if we were all leaders, who would follow? Wouldn't there be chaos if we all tried to lead at the same time? Well, that's where knowing your lane comes in. In a race, you need to stay in your lane. In life and leadership, your lane represents your role, your area, your zone.

You've probably heard the old adage about "too many cooks in the kitchen." I get it. But that's only true if all the cooks are working on the same dish or getting in each other's way. The real problem is not too many cooks. The real problem is when one cook is interfering with the other cook's job, when the cooks don't stay in their lane.

Think of it this way. You have to feed a thousand people for lunch tomorrow. You don't want to be the only cook in the kitchen! You need people in charge of different areas. And then you need those cooks to do their job and stay in their lane! You actually need more cooks in the kitchen. You need more leaders in your church. And everyone needs to "stay in their lane."

Some pastors think they have too many "leaders" in their church already because there are competing systems, dueling personalities, and chaos. But those problems aren't caused by too much leadership. It's usually a lack of clear leadership, failure of people staying in their lanes, or areas of giftedness, that cause conflict.

First Corinthians 14:26-33 tells us that the church in Corinth had a problem. They actually had a lot of problems. When they got together to worship, it was chaotic. It seems that people wanted to speak at the same time. So, while one was delivering the sermon, another person would stand up and begin to speak in tongues. Not to be outdone, someone else would chime in with prophesy, while someone else would begin singing a song—all right in the middle of the service and all at the same time. And evidently, when questioned about the wisdom of this chaotic disorder of service, some would try to blame it on the Spirit. Can't you hear a Corinthian brother or sister say, "Hey, when God moves, I can't hold back. I just have to sing!"

So the Apostle Paul steps in and brings down the hammer. He says, "You can all prophesy one at a time so that everyone can learn and be encouraged. The spirits of prophets are under the control of the prophets. God isn't a God of disorder but of peace"

(1 Cor 14:31-33 CEB). In other words, hold your horses, people. Take turns and stay in your lane!

In Ephesians 4, we are given a short list of different kinds of leaders in the church. There are apostles, prophets, evangelists, pastors, and teachers. Each of these has a "lane," an area of expertise and responsibility. Now look at the end game. They are to equip God's people for what? For ministry. They aren't supposed to *do* all the ministry. They are to *equip* others to do ministry too. So that means every Christ follower, every Christian is to be in ministry. It doesn't mean every Christian is a pastor or prophet. That may not be their lane. But every Christian is a minister, preferably being equipped to discover and engage in a particular niche or lane for which they are uniquely qualified. Churches need pastoral leadership and lay leadership to know their own lane and to respect and appreciate other lanes too. Leaders need to learn to work together in a partnership. That's the body of Christ in action, working together in rhythm and respect.

What's your lane? Well, that's what you need to find out. Some clues are your personality, interests, and life experiences. What are you good at? What things excite you? What do you see happening in your church or community or the world and say, "Somebody ought to do something about that!" These questions are clues to your "lane" and where you will be the happiest and most effective for the kingdom.

Somehow in America, many Christians have gotten the idea that showing up to a church service fulfills their Christian duty. But according to Ephesians that's a ridiculous idea! You aren't meant to just be a passenger on the boat. You are meant to help row the boat! By the way, have you noticed that when people are busy rowing the boat there isn't much time for rocking the boat?

Many pastors spend all their time *doing* ministry. That's not a biblical model. Many laypeople spend all their time either on boards and committees or just attending church. That's not a biblical model either. The biblical model is for every believer to be in a lane, in a ministry (Eph 4:12).

Find your lane. Then lead. And stay in your lane.

Every church and every horse needs a leader. Be a leader.

Born or Trained?

Clinton Anderson is one of my favorite horse trainers. I like his Aussie accent, down-to-earth humor, and ability to break complex behavior into manageable steps. Clinton brought his Downunder Horsemanship clinic to a nearby town, and I jumped at the chance to see him work his magic in person. As he opened the seminar, he addressed the crowd with this question: "How many of you would say you are natural horse people? Working with horses just comes naturally to you." Of the five-hundred-plus people present, only a few raised their hands, much to our envy. But Clinton's response made the rest of us feel better.

With a mischievous smile, he said, "Well, get out of here! The rest of us can't stand people like you!" And the whole crowd roared with laughter, even the now sheepish ones who had raised their hands.

Horsemanship can be taught. And so can leadership. Yes, some people seem to be naturals. There probably are a few natural-born horsemen and natural-born leaders. But not many. So, what about the rest of us? We can learn. We can improve. We can find our area of influence and grow as leaders.

In fact, there are some real advantages to NOT being a natural-born leader. Have you noticed that many natural-born athletes or musicians or mathematicians or even preachers have difficulty explaining how they do what they do to others? They can't explain it because it comes intuitively. "I don't know how I hit that note. I just do it." "I don't know how I gather a crowd. I just do it."

Prodigies are a small population, especially in the leadership world. Most of us are not natural-born leaders. Most of us must learn the hard way by making mistakes. We must learn how to be good leaders. It's a fact that every church, horse, business, and family needs a leader. It's a job in high demand. But many people count themselves out before they even try. Leadership can be learned. You can be a leader. Actually, the case can be made that you already are a leader in some sphere of influence. But if you aren't aware that you are a leader already, you probably aren't doing your best at it.

Seri questioned my leadership by acting out when she sensed a leadership vacuum. Churches can react in much the same way. They experience chaos and conflict when leadership is unclear or people are out of their lanes.

Read, study, and practice being a leader. Find your lane.

What excites you? What frustrates you? What needs to be done that no one else seems to see? These may be clues into how God has wired you and what your particular lane looks like.

"Too many cooks in the kitchen" really means that people are out of their lanes. In the 100-meter dash, if you get out of your lane you're disqualified because that interferes with the other runners. In churches, it's usually not quite that clear. We probably wish we could blow a whistle and make problematic participants sit on the bench. But we often only know someone is out of their lane by the damage that's happening in their wake.

Your church, your business, and your family need leaders. Not a Lone Ranger or Superman who single-handedly saves the day. Get over that idea. You're most effective as a leader when you use your skills and talents to help others find their lane and respect and encourage those around you to do the same.

There's often a silent question asked within organizations and teams: "Who's in charge here?" That's what Seri was asking me. This question often arises when the leadership is struggling with ambiguity or alignment. However, you can make the confusion worse. If you have to remind people verbally that you are the leader, then you're in a lot of trouble already! Good leaders don't rely on titles, rules, or manipulation. Good leaders demonstrate competence within their lane by example and by helping those following to get better at being leaders themselves.

Questions for Discussion:

1. What is a key take-away for you from this chapter?

2. Do you agree with the statement that anyone can and should be a leader?

3. Have you accepted your role as leader in your spheres of influence?

4. Have you ever seen the result of "too many cooks in the kitchen?" Looking back, do you think the resulting chaos was because of too many leaders, or that the leaders weren't staying in their "lanes"?

5. How do you think pastoral leadership and lay leadership in the church can work better together in partnership?

6. How would these same lessons apply in your home and job?

7. What would it look like if you embraced your role as a leader? In your home? Your church? Your business?

8. What's one practice or habit you would like to improve in your leadership skills? For example, read a particular book for self-improvement, attend a seminar, learn to use a new app on your smart phone, or find a life coach.

Chapter 2
THE PATIENCE POLE

To change your horse you must first change yourself.

—Clinton Anderson

Be still, and know that I am God!

—Psalm 46:10a (NRSV)

Chasing Deer

I t's a warm day, almost perfect. The sun is shining gently, and there's a cool breeze in our faces. Seri and I are doing one of our favorite things—running. We're out in the woods, crossing streams, dodging trees, running fast. Of course, when I say running fast, I mean Seri is running fast and I'm holding on for dear life. I'm a paradox of laughing out loud one second and cringing in terror the next because—I may not have mentioned this before—I'm really not a great rider. But I'm learning.

We crossed a stream, and I looked up as movement caught my eye ahead of us. Deer! Three beautiful does were apparently alerted by our splashing. They stopped and we stopped. Seri arched her neck and perked her ears forward as she examined these intruders on her trail. The deer were more inquisitive than startled. But after a long stare-down, one of them bolted and the others followed. With no plan whatsoever, I squeezed with my knees and made a kissing sound, which is my signal to Seri to run like a rocket. I yelled, "Let's get 'em, girl!" And we were off! Ha! Truthfully, the deer were never in any danger of being caught, and I sure didn't have a plan for what to do if I caught one, despite my bold and impulsive declaration.

But it was a fun race for us, and perhaps the deer had a good chuckle too.

I knew this trail well. If the deer continued their trajectory, they would intersect with Seri and me in about fifty yards. So instead of a direct pursuit through the trees, we bolted up the track. Sure enough, the three deer spilled out of the woods right in our path, and the pursuit picked up more speed. Seri had the idea now. This was a chase! I'm sure she had no better clue than I did what we would do with a deer if we caught it, but logic didn't allow those calculations in the heat of the moment. We were running hard and fast, and that's what Seri was born to do.

I laughed at a fleeting thought about the Narnians chasing the White Stag in *The Lion, the Witch, and the Wardrobe*. If you caught him, he would grant your wishes. The White Stag was never caught in Narnia, and in a few seconds, I found out why. Those does with their graceful bounds looked back at us, seemed to grin mischievously, and then shifted into a warp speed that Seri and I could not match. I smiled at their beauty and amazing speed as they flew into the thick woods safely out of reach. Seri seemed satisfied. The intruders had been expelled, and she could resume as the undisputed Queen of the Wood.

Like those deer, Seri was born to run. And when she runs, it's like music. Oh, I wish you could see her run! It's like poetry.

It's like a symphony building to its crescendo. You don't have to be a horse person to appreciate the fluid beauty of movement. You can see such beauty when a wave crashes into white foam on the rocks, or when a hawk tucks in for her dive, or when an athlete at the top of his or her

"Like flying without wings"

game performs at the pinnacle of human ability. It's hard to describe the beauty of a horse in motion unless you've seen an Arabian horse swallow up the ground in strides that seem to barely touch the earth. It's like flying without wings—neck arched, tail held high! And to be on the back of a galloping horse (and not fall off) is an honor. When you fall off, it really doesn't feel like an honor. But when things work just right, there is a partnership and a friendship that is forged between human and horse at speed. Seri was born to run.

But I'll tell you what she was not born for, what aggravates her, irritates her, and goes against her grain: standing still. As much as she loves to run, in an equal measure she seems to despise standing still. She will huff and blow and swat her tale and stomp her feet. She'll toss her head and pull at the rope as if to say, "Why are we just standing here? We're wasting time! We need to move!"

With life, as with horses, there's a time to run and there's a time to stand still. Seri can't run all the time or in every circumstance and condition. Sometimes she has to walk. And sometimes she has to be still. And so we practice. We practice standing still.

Leadership is about movement, helping a group move from point A to point B. But sometimes leadership is also about standing still. Slowing down. Stopping to listen, learn, and evaluate. Sometimes leadership is moving, but sometimes it's waiting. I can relate to Seri's impatience. Perhaps you can too. I like to go fast. In my own direction. At my pace.

Seri comes by this desire to run naturally. While all horses, as mammals, are warm-blooded, we mean something different by a "hot-blooded" horse. Horses are categorized informally by their temperament. Arabians and Thoroughbreds are called "hot-blooded" because of their energy. They are ready to go!

Big draft horses like the Clydesdale and Belgians are never invited to the Kentucky Derby. They are considered "cold-blooded" because of their slower, calmer nature. They can run if they must, but they'd much rather take a nap. You can probably think of people—family members, co-workers, church members—who might also be categorized as either hot-blooded or cold-blooded. Waiting is hard for hot-blooded people!

Seri is an Arabian and fully owns that hot-blooded temperament. She strives to run. She enjoys running. In fact, it seems like she never gets tired. We both love running through wooded trails. Running fast and far is fun to her. But sometimes she needs to stand still, like when I'm getting on her back. Or where the terrain makes it dangerous to run. Or when she just needs to listen to me for directions. She needs to stand still.

Learning to Wait

Clinton Anderson, an Austrailian-born horseman who now lives in the U.S. and has a popular equine television program on

Fox Sports Net,[1] sells an interesting training device called a "patience pole." It's a simple pole with a swivel at the top. The horse is tied to this pole and can move, but only in short circles, so it can't get tangled or hurt itself. Even the most hot-blooded, impatient horse finally discovers that it can only move in tight circles,

Seri used to be afraid of water but now enjoys a cool dip

so it might as well settle down, think about things, and become a cooperative citizen. This isn't a punishment tool. It's a training tool. But the horse probably doesn't realize that at first. It feels like punishment, so it resists until it gets tired, and then the horse rests, listens, and waits.

How about you? Has God ever attached you to a Patience Pole? You want to run, but you're forced to wait. It feels like punishment, restriction, time-out, or the penalty box. You're waiting for a decision. Waiting for direction. Waiting for a sign.

Learning to wait

Waiting for an answer to your prayer. Sometimes it feels like God is not listening or has even abandoned you. But perhaps God is

---

1. Downunderhorsemanship.com is Clinton Anderson's website.

really just trying to get your attention. To get you to be still and listen and learn.

So here's a question for you: How long can you wait?

How long can you wait before you get anxious, confused, frustrated, afraid, or bitter? How long can you continue to work hard without recognition? How long can you stand true to your convictions while being misunderstood? How long can you wait for slower or meandering people to catch up with you?

How long can you wait for God to answer before you start off with your own plan?

Don't be too worried if you answered these questions with "Not very long!" We're always leaders-in-training.

The ability to wait is a sign of maturity, intelligence, and leadership. Waiting will test you. It will stretch you. Leaders must learn to wait if we are to be effective.

When our kids were infants in the crib, I can remember the blood-curdling screams that meant either "feed me," "change me," or "don't leave me." Training babies to sleep through the night is not for the timid. It can be quite nerve-racking. We'd tuck ours in, make sure they were clean and dry, and then walk out of the room. And then the crying would start. And not just crying—they sounded like screams of desperation! To the baby brain, it's as if the loving parental unit drops into the abyss when they are out of sight. We played a little game of peek-a-boo with ours, to show them that walking out of the room didn't mean we dropped off the edge of the earth. Did it work? Well, not at first. There was still a lot of crying, but eventually it did.

It takes a while to learn things sometimes. You see, babies are among the least mature of our species, with politicians claiming the number one slot. Ha! Just kidding, politicians.

It takes time to learn to...wait. In fact, attention span and the amount of time a child (or adult) can wait are indicators of a maturity level. When God is silent or when you don't know what to do, how long can you wait?

Teachers and Tests

Here's another analogy. Have you noticed that teachers are usually silent during tests? When I was in the fifth grade, some adults thought that my energy was guided by a mischievous streak. Ha! Some would say I never outgrew this prankishness. I remember sitting in the classroom of Mr. Williams, a teacher who I really liked. We were taking a test one day, and I became stuck on one of the questions. It was a multiple-choice question, and the more I read over the answers, the more (a), (b), and (c) seemed to be confusingly similar. As I muddled and mused about the merits of just guessing a letter, suddenly an idea came to me. I won't claim this as divine inspiration, but it was so innovative, so new, so bold that I felt adrenaline course through my veins. The idea seemed genius, but did I have the boldness to pull it off? Throwing caution to the wind, I mustered my courage and raised my hand to ask my question and activate my scheme. Mr. Williams was huddled over a pile of papers on his desk and only looked up occasionally to make sure that "all eyes are on your own paper." He saw my hand on one of his glances up and said distractedly, "Yes?"

Here was the moment of truth. With as much nonchalance as I could muster, I said, "I'm having trouble with number five. Is the answer (b)?" Then before anyone, including Mr. Williams, realized what was happening, he replied in the same distracted voice, "No, it's (c)."

Tick…tick…tick. It took about three long seconds before Mr. Williams and the class recognized the subterfuge I had accomplished. Everyone laughed, including good Mr. Williams, and for a few short minutes I was the acknowledged hero of fifth grade. Of course, this led to multiple imitators and copycat attempts, but none achieved the same magnificent result.

Mr. Williams, like most teachers, remained silent during tests. Because that's what teachers do. They teach during the teaching time but are silent during the test time. You see, good teachers don't give tests to hurt you. Good teachers give tests so you and they can find out what you know and what you don't know. Then they can teach you what you don't know.

God is a good teacher. And because of this, God is often silent during a test. It doesn't mean God doesn't like you. It doesn't mean God is trying to fail you. It doesn't mean God has abandoned you. It's just a test. It's not meant to hurt you but to help you know what you know and don't know. Then you can learn what you need to know.

Sounds reasonable—except when it is happening to you. And it happens to all of us. Waiting is a test. But when it does happen to us, tests aren't merely theoretical. They are real and often painful. In fact, tests are hard to recognize when you're in them because the word *test* doesn't describe the pain or fear or desperation you may feel.

A great song from my youth, "Back in the Furnace," was written by Steve Camp. The first verse includes these particularly compelling lines:

Under the hands of a loving Father, he is refining me
    perfectly.
And the fire consumes not my person, it's burning away my
    impurities.

Then, the chorus underscores this metaphor of "the furnace" where we are tested, thirsty, hungry for a friend. I still find myself singing the chorus when being trained on God's "patience pole." Waiting and testing are not bad for us, but they can feel exactly like abandonment and condemnation. Leaders need the ability to wait, and it's equally important for a leader to help others to wait in healthy rather than anxious ways.

In the first few years of launching a new congregation, my emotions fluctuated between extremely stressed to totally exhilarated. Launching a new church is much like starting a new business. With approximately an 80 percent failure rate for start-ups, there are ups and downs and acute moments when you don't know if this idea is going to work. We drew people who had never been to church, who would attend, get to know Jesus, and gradually experience a changed heart and life. That was the rewarding part of the effort. The stressful part had to do with systems, finances, finding new places to meet, and wondering if people were going to show up.

Lyle Schaller, whom *Christianity Today* called "the dean of church consultants,"[2] observed that if a new church didn't get to an average attendance of at least two hundred in the first year, then statistically it probably never would. (Church consultants observe that a church with fewer than two hundred members is

2. David Neff, "CT's Modest Dynamic Duo," *Christianity Today,* March 14, 2007.

not financially sustainable.) Those words troubled me. When I went to bed at night, I stared at the ceiling and in my imagination would see the number *200* hovering over me. Thankfully, perhaps miraculously, we reached that milestone. We grew to two hundred and a little more, and I had dreams of being off to the races! Momentum was with us, and good things were happening. I felt the sky was the limit.

And then we got stuck. Nothing bad happened. We just stopped growing. So I tried new things, called my coach, prayed, strategized, and worked harder. Actually, that's probably my go-to solution: work harder and faster. I tried to preach better and make the music better and strengthen our systems, which were all necessary and good tactics. But it didn't work. It seemed no matter what I tried, we couldn't get unstuck and growing again.

Some people are critical of large churches and accuse them of an unhealthy interest in growing the numbers. Perhaps some leaders are tainted by self-aggrandizement. But some church leaders overreact to this flaw and say with a bit of pride, "Oh, we don't count our attendance. We just love who shows up." If you want to rib the critics a little, just ask politely if they count the offering. The answer is sure to come back in the affirmative, and then you can innocently ask, "Why? You don't care more about money than people, do you?" Ha! (There's my mischievous streak again.)

But I don't think that's where I was. Whether launching a new church or rebooting an old one, we know there are people, certainly a majority, in our area, who are unfamiliar with any church and need a life-changing relationship with Jesus. With priorities clear, we know those "numbers" are really individuals far from God, and our calling, our primary purpose, is to reach them. We aim to help those folks get connected to God. In the process of reaching and training, we will get stuck many times. Plateaus are a natural and inevitable part of growth. They're not exciting. We don't want to stay stuck forever, but plateaus can be our friend.

I remember coming home discouraged one day. Instead of going inside the house, I sat in my truck and prayed. "God, what am I doing wrong?" There wasn't a clap of thunder, and no hand appeared writing on the wall with the hidden solution to my problem. In hindsight, I'm relieved, because handwriting on the wall happened only once in ancient history, and the message was "You're doomed!" (Read Daniel 5.)

Without trying to sound dramatic, I sensed God speaking to me: "Stay the course. This is a season." And then I felt a sense of peace. Nothing changed except my attitude. Oh, I still wanted to run and grow, but now I relaxed a bit more. I didn't know about the Patience Pole at that time, but I was on one. And I stopped struggling, pawing, pulling at the bit, trying to run ahead.

Have you ever been restricted by a Patience Pole? If not, you will be! You will be tested. The lesson of the Patience Pole is learning how to wait calmly. I'd like to say that everyone eventually learns this lesson and passes this test. But that's not accurate. As a leader, there are no guarantees. Not everyone goes home with a participation trophy in life. You can fail this test for a lot of reasons: pride, insecurity, stubbornness, arrogance, fear. And there's a lot at stake. Sometimes our families, churches, or organizations suffer if its leaders refuse to learn and to wait. One extreme outcome for not learning to wait is being disqualified as a leader entirely. Sound harsh? How useful can a staff person be if they don't listen and take direction? How useful can we be if we don't wait and listen for God's still, quiet voice (1 Kgs 19:12 CEB) but are always running ahead with our own plans?

Saul Can't Wait (1 Samuel 13)

In 1 Samuel 13 we find Saul in trouble. He knew it, too. After all, he was the first king of a small Middle-East nation trying to find its purpose and identity. His country was surrounded by attacking enemy forces, and his small army was outnumbered. The enemy's army is described this way: "The Philistines also were gathered to fight against Israel. They brought thirty thousand chariots with them, six thousand cavalry, and as many soldiers as there is sand on the seashore to fight Israel" (1 Sam 13:5a CEB).

I imagine Saul saying to himself, "No wonder I got this job; no one else wanted it!" But Israel wasn't defenseless. They had a lot going for them. Saul had highly motivated soldiers, and a son and heir to the throne who was proving to be an outstanding warrior. But mainly Israel had God. The Lord was speaking directly to a prophet named Samuel, and every time Saul obeyed what God said through Samuel, everything turned out right, no matter the odds.

But when the Israeli army saw the numbers and technology of the enemy, they panicked. They forgot about their loyalty to Saul, Samuel, and even God, and they began to flee for their lives. Saul knew he was in trouble. Perhaps this was his first major crisis of leadership. Perhaps his advisors were demanding that he do something. Saul knew he was in trouble. What he didn't know was that he was also in a test. He was waiting on the Patience Pole.

Samuel instructed him clearly to wait for the prophet's arrival at Gilgal before proceeding. Samuel would sacrifice and pray to the Lord. So Saul waited...and waited...and waited. He waited seven days…and then he broke. He made the sacrifices himself, clearly disobeying God's instruction in the Torah. He got out of his lane. And because of this violation, Saul was disqualified from being king and his dynasty would no longer rule in Israel. Samuel rebukes Saul upon his arrival:

> How stupid of you to have broken the commands the LORD your God gave you!" Samuel told Saul. "The LORD would have established your rule over Israel forever, but now your rule won't last. The LORD will search for a man following the LORD's own heart, and the LORD will commission him as leader over God's people, because you didn't keep the LORD's command. (1 Sam 13:13-14 CEB)

That's a clear (and sad) example of cause and effect. You disobeyed. You didn't wait. You got out of your lane, and the consequences are severe. As leaders, we're a little sympathetic to Saul here. "Come on, he waited seven days. The prophet was a no-show. He had to do something."

Yes, he had to do something. We must do *something*. But one of those options of "doing something" is to wait. To be still. To listen. This may seem harsh to us, but remember, the greater the leadership position, the greater the responsibility. Don't miss the lesson here: When God says "wait," God means wait.

The Patience Pole is a tool and a test, but it can feel like punishment or abandonment. The next time you're forced to wait—if you can recognize that it is God, rather than a fallible human cause—take a deep breath and say, "Okay, I'm on the patience pole. This is a test. Help me wait, listen, and obey you, Lord. Amen."

Questions for Discussion

1. What is a key take-away from this chapter?

2. Can you remember a time when you were made to wait? How did you handle it?

3. Would you describe your personality as "hot-blooded" or "cold-blooded"?

4. When you are moving slow, do you learn and rest, or do you get anxious or frustrated?

5. What lessons might God be trying to teach you while you are on the "patience pole"?

6. How do you respond when your Teacher (God) is silent during a test?

7. Can you recall a time when you felt you were feeling the heat, and being "refined" as expressed in the Steve Camp song "Back in the Furnace"?

CHARGE WHAT SCARES YOU

Advance and retreat was one of the first lessons taught to me by horses and I was later to discover that it works well with people too.

—*Monty Roberts*

Courage is being scared to death, but saddling up anyway.

—*John Wayne*

There's a season for everything and a time for every matter under the heavens. . . . a time for embracing and a time for avoiding embraces.

—*Ecclesiastes 3:1, 5 (CEB)*

Water Dragons and Metal Monsters

Seri is a warhorse. She is a descendant of a proud line of warriors. Her ancestors have charged into battle, toppled kingdoms, and fought desert lions. She can trace her lineage back to King Solomon's stables, so she is not intimidated by royalty. She is noble, strong, and brave.

27

Except when she's not.

She can be a downright chicken about the silliest things. "So you can chase a lion, but a plastic bag makes you wet your pants. Real brave, Seri."

But that's how horses are. The same horse who faces a panther to defend her herd might also spook and run for the hills when confronted by a mud puddle. Horses are prey animals rather than predators. Prey animals are also called "flight animals," which means their primary defense mechanism is to run away from what scares them. They are wired differently from the animals familiar to most of us, such as dogs and cats. Dogs and cats are predators. Humans are predators. Horses are prey. Predators and prey think differently. They are motivated by different things, and they look at the world differently.

Predator: "I'm looking for something to eat."

Prey: "I'm looking for something that might eat me."

The first instinct of prey animals when encountering something unfamiliar, questionable, or spooky is to change zip codes in a hurry! They get out of there. "What's that? A squirrel! Best run away uncontrollably in a panic!"

So, if we're going to learn from horses, we need to understand how they think differently, and learn to speak a bit of their language.

One day, I took a ride down memory lane. I loaded Seri up on the trailer and headed south about two hours to the area where I grew up. I hadn't visited the old stomping grounds since I was a kid, and I was excited to ride the dirt roads where I played as a boy. I had a great time reminiscing that day. Some of the landscape had changed, but some brought back sweet memories of boyhood.

I saw the old barn where my brother and I played our favorite make-believe game: "Man-eating Fish." Tractors and equipment were parked in a line under the shed, and the game was to cross from one side of the building to the other without touching the ground. If you touched the ground, you fell into the man-eating fish and had to start over. I cringe now as I think back at some of the daredevil leaps we took from tractor to harrow to combine. I imagine getting to heaven one day and meeting the angels who kept us crazy kids from killing ourselves. I'll probably owe them a big apology for making them work overtime.

Seri, on the other hand, didn't enjoy the day nearly as much, primarily because of the two "monsters" she encountered. Close to the house where I grew up was a field of peanuts under irrigation. In the South, many of the irrigation systems are enormous metal tubes spraying water with a loud hissing sound. Seri seemed to think this contraption was an angry water dragon threatening to attack and eat her. One of the horse-related sayings about problems that I've picked up goes like this: "Everything is training." So when we encounter something that Seri is afraid of, I just consider it training and try to take the time to show her that there is nothing to fear. We do this by gradually moving closer and closer to the thing causing fear. She gets to see and smell and listen to the foreign object and discover for herself that this thing that spooked her is really not a threat.

But this particular situation was a challenge. The irrigation system was moving, hissing, and shooting water, and this monster wasn't backing down. We spent about twenty minutes moving closer and then backing up, moving closer and backing up, getting a little closer on each advance. Eventually we got to the point where the water could hit us, and I decided to call it a win.

Seri was relieved and ready to get out of there. She had faced her fears, but I didn't want to push our luck with the water-spewing leviathan.

This technique is actually a form of systematic desensitization used by counselors and psychologists to help people with their traumas and phobias. The system is designed to gradually face fears in small portions. The "desensitization" occurs in human and beast when we are gradually less afraid because we're convinced there is no real threat.

Siri studies the "Water Dragon"

For instance, if someone is afraid of clowns (and why have clowns gotten so creepy lately?), the client might be led through some breathing exercises to relax and then shown a picture of a clown. As the anxiety level rises, the picture is taken away. The client might be asked to rate their level of anxiety on a scale from one to ten. "Whew, that was a seven! I hate clowns!"

The exercise would be repeated: look at the clown picture, give a level of anxiety reading, breathe to calm back down, and repeat. Eventually, the picture of the clown is not nearly as new and terrifying but becomes mundane and boring. When the client reaches a manageable level of anxiety, the heat is turned up again. This time a clown doll may be brought in. The anxiety level probably shoots back up, and the process starts again from the beginning. The grand finale, of course, culminates when the client hugs a real clown, falls in love with it, and runs off to join the circus.

A more extreme method of desensitization is called "flooding." Take the same scenario of the client afraid of clowns, but this time skip the slow, systematic treatment. Instead, lock the client in a room full of terrifying clowns until the client either dies of fright or gets over it! (If you go to a therapist who tries to persuade you to try flooding, find a new therapist.) But there is a moderate approach that is sometimes used in training horses.

There's an exciting horse-training championship competition called "Road to the Horse" that employs desensitization. Three talented horse trainers are chosen to go head-to-head in a two-day event. Each trainer is assigned an untrained colt they've never met. These young horses have never been ridden and are essentially wild. It's amazing to see these horse whisperers take a wild horse on day one and be able to ride it, stand in the saddle, and even crank a chainsaw while standing horseback by day two!

How do they do it? A common first step, mentioned in chapter 1, involves moving the horse's feet and establishing the trainer as herd leader. While the horse is made to move his feet in a round pen, other possible fears are introduced, such as an umbrella, beach ball, and crumpled tarp. Thus the trainer is doing several things at once: establishing himself or herself as herd leader, building trust, and desensitizing the horse to spooky objects. The horse may balk at the umbrella and jump over the tarp at first, but begins to see these objects as harmless and ignores them after a couple of laps. That's what you want—a horse that pays attention to you and trusts your leadership more than it fears the unknown.

During my day riding down Memory Lane, Seri's quota of fear was not yet complete. On the way back to the trailer, we retraced our tracks down a red dirt road. It was long, narrow, and straight with unclimbable ditches on both sides. I mention this because I looked up and saw something barreling down on us about a half mile away. It was a large cotton sprayer approaching. Imagine a tractor but stretched twelve feet or more in the air. Cotton grows tall so the equipment used to work it must be taller. This vehicle is so tall you could probably drive a small car under it. It was tall, wide, and moving fast. Seri noticed it too and must have wondered what new monster this was. I felt the tension rise in her body as she became more nervous. Actually, my anxiety was rising too—not because I was afraid of the tractor but because I was on a nervous horse about to be run down by a huge machine and I had nowhere to go. Fortunately, the driver finally saw us and slowed down about fifty yards away. But by this time, Seri was experiencing real panic. And I couldn't blame her. The tractor was tall, loud, and wide, taking up most of the narrow dirt road. The considerate driver finally stopped about ten yards from us, but Seri's nerves could take no more.

As a prey animal, her first instinct is to run. I can only imagine the terror produced by this huge monster. I quickly tried to think of good options, while Seri spun underneath me, eyes wide with panic. I could barely keep her under some semblance of control. This situation moved from dicey to dangerous.

We usually have at least four directions to choose from: forward, backward, left or right. Left and right were not options because of the high ditch walls. Backward seemed a poor option because our pace would slow down the tractor for miles, and I didn't want to reinforce Seri's fear by running away. That left one direction—forward. So we did something a bit counterintuitive. We charged. I think I actually yelled, "CHARGE!" to brace our nerves and stir our courage. Seri objected and quaked with fear, but that's what we did. There were only a few yards of opening between the side of the tractor and the ditch, so I pointed Seri's head at the opening and squeezed hard with my legs. And Seri charged!

She charged the monster that was terrifying her. She charged something that she had never experienced before. She charged and got past it. Because sometimes you must make the counter-intuitive move. Sometimes you have to charge what scares you.

Let me hit the Pause button here for a few leadership questions:

1. As a leader, what are you afraid of?
2. Does anything have you paralyzed?
3. How do you typically deal with things you've never faced before?

Many of us fall into paralysis when facing something we fear. It might be an uncertain future or too many options or a fear of making the wrong decision. To make matters a bit more complicated, sometimes it's difficult to tell the difference between *waiting* (as we discussed in chapter 2) and *paralysis*. What is the difference? When we wait too long where action is needed, your organization, team, or church experiences paralysis.

Advance and Retreat

The option of charging or chasing what scares you is not completely out of line with the way horses think. Monty Roberts tells how the early western Native American tribes captured horses. It's a method he calls "Advance and Retreat."

Members of the tribe would chase a herd of wild horses they wanted to capture and then suddenly stop. When the horses realized their pursuers had stopped chasing them, they stopped too and turned around to get a look. Then the tribe would retreat. They would slowly begin to back up. And amazingly, the horses would start to follow. Why would the horses do that? Why would they start moving toward the very thing that was chasing them? Possibly, as prey animals, they want to keep an eye on a potential threat. There's something about a horse's brain that responds to pressure and the release of pressure. Being chased (the advance) adds pressure and the horses move away from it. When pressure is released (the retreat), the horses change direction. It's like the ebb and flow of the tide.

Then the tribe would turn back toward the herd and begin the chase again. This would be repeated; advance and retreat, advance and retreat, until the cunning tribe could lead the herd of horses into a canyon and close the gap.

James Dobson doesn't use equine terminology in his book *Love Must Be Tough*,[1] but he refers to the same principle and how it sometimes plays out in relationships. Suppose a spouse has an affair. The other spouse finds out about the indiscretion but wants to keep the marriage together. What are the options? Dobson suggests that the best response is counterintuitive (and reminiscent of

---

1. See James Dobson, *Love Must Be Tough: New Hope for Marriages in Crisis* (Carol Stream, IL: Tyndale, 2007).

"Advance and Retreat"). If the offended spouse chases hard toward the other spouse, placing blame on oneself and making promises of better conditions at home, the offending spouse is likely to run farther away. The offender is repelled by the chase. But if the offended spouse doesn't chase, there's a better chance of reconciliation. Dobson recommends assuming an emotional position that might translate something like this from the offended spouse:

Obviously, I'm deeply hurt by your actions. I would like to work together to save our marriage and reach a place of trust and commitment. But we need a new day; a new way of treating each other. I'm not willing to just look the other way and maintain the status quo. I would like to work with you to save our marriage. But I'm not willing to be the only one working. If you would like to join me, then let's work together. But if not, then I'll let you go in peace.

This approach to reconciliation is not a trick or reverse psychology used to manipulate someone into staying. When used as a genuine response, the message is very powerful, but there are no guarantees. You've probably noticed in life that we can only change ourselves. We have very little power to change anyone else. We tend to repel others if we chase or pressure too hard. But our position is attractive when it comes from a genuine place of strength. "I'm going to get closer to Christ. That's the best thing I can do. I want to invite you to do the same, but regardless of what you decide, I'm going closer to Jesus." Advance adds pressure. Retreat removes pressure.

In an earlier experience, Seri and I encountered another example of this counterintuitive equine thinking. My brother Brad and I were meeting at my parents' house for some good home cooking. I brought Seri with me so we could hit some dirt roads after lunch. Brad doesn't ride horses, but he does ride a bike, so he grabbed one out of the garage and said, "Let's go!" I wasn't quite sure how Seri would react but was interested in finding out. After all, "Everything is training." We started off with Seri and I in the lead and Brad and the bike following slowly behind us. This was a mistake, and you can probably guess why. Seri felt chased. She pranced and arched her neck with the whites in her eyes showing. She wondered what this strange device was that pursued her. I told Brad, "Hey, let's try something different. Get in front of us, and let us *chase* you."

Seri wasn't too thrilled when the bike pulled up beside her, but when Brad pulled ahead, she relaxed. The contraption that had been chasing her was now running away from her. After about thirty minutes, she was at ease with the bike riding beside, and we had a great ride together. Sometimes we have to chase what scares us. Face it, stare it down, and charge.

John Wayne is credited with saying "Courage is being scared to death, but saddling up anyway." You're going to face fears as a leader. Fear of the future, of failure, of leading the wrong way. Fear can paralyze leaders. Sure, there's a time to wait, but there's also a time to charge what you are afraid of. And many times this just doesn't feel natural. It may even be the opposite of what you feel like doing.

Bad Cycles Make a Rut (Judges 6)

Gideon was an unlikely leader, much less hero. But he became both. In the book of Judges, the people of Israel are living with leader turnover. Moses and Joshua are long gone, and a series of "judges" (chieftains) periodically rise up to get the budding nation of Israel out of their pattern of self-destruction. That pattern is described at least eight times: "the Israelites again did things that the LORD saw as evil" (Judg 4:1 CEB).

We've seen what happens when there is a vacuum of righteous leadership. Horses get horsey, families fall apart, the national moral compass becomes skewed, and societies lose their identity and collective relationship with God. Faithful, strong, intentional leadership is important to God's people. And Israel didn't always have this kind of leadership.

According to the authors who compiled the books of Deuteronomy through Kings, a predictable pattern was established: A leader rises to help the tribes return to the Lord. With some leaders, things go well for a while—until the people turn away from God to worship idols and follow their own selfish desires. As a consequence, God allows an enemy to attack or conquer the tribes. Over and over this cycle seems to repeat itself in the Old Testament. The tribes are at a low point in the cycle when we meet Gideon in Judges 6. "The Israelites did things that the LORD saw as evil, and the LORD handed them over to the Midianites for seven years" (Judg 6:1 CEB).

The story continues as an angel approaches Gideon and offers a seemingly ironic greeting: "The LORD is with you, mighty warrior!" (Judg 6:12 CEB). It doesn't seem like the Lord is anywhere close by because Israel is worshipping Baal again instead of, or in addition to, the Lord. As C. S. Lewis once said, "By blending the lie with some truth, they made the lie stronger."

The greeting is also ironic because the "mighty warrior" Gideon has never fought a battle in his life. Gideon may be thinking, "So, no offense, Mr. Angel, but I'm not sure who you're talking to when you say 'Mighty Warrior.'"

But Gideon seems to be a realist in his response: "With all due respect, my Lord, if the Lord is with us, why has all this happened to us? Where are all his amazing works that our ancestors recounted to us, saying, 'Didn't the Lord bring us up from Egypt?' But now the Lord has abandoned us and allowed Midian to overpower us" (Judg 6:13 CEB).

Aren't you glad this is in the Bible? Haven't you felt like this at times? I sure have. "Lord, if you're with me, why is this happening? If you love me, why didn't you step in and do something?"

You've probably never faced an invading army, but you may have faced cancer or divorce or your kids losing their minds and doing crazy stuff. "With all due respect, Lord, if you're here and you love us, then why are we going through this mess?"

Those are honest questions—and good ones. From all the evidence around Gideon, it must seem that either God isn't there or God doesn't care. Neither of these things is true, but Gideon can't see the big picture. He can see the pieces but can't connect the dots. In the midst of threat and chaos, it helps to remember that we have limited vision too. We see our culture and circumstances from our standpoint. We are in the middle of it and often can't see the forest for the trees. God is above it and sees it all. God knows the end of the story.

But notice this: God doesn't answer Gideon's questions. Instead, he gives Gideon an assignment and promises to be with him.

"Go and rescue Israel from the power of Midian...I'm with you...." (Judg 6:14, 16 NLT).

Even though Gideon asked good questions, God didn't answer his questions.

Even though you ask good questions, God might not give you the answers either: "Why did my child die?" "Why did my spouse leave?" "Why did that car wreck happen?" Why? Perhaps, in some cases, God knows we need something other than the answers we expect.

We think we need the answer to "why," but what we really need is the same thing Gideon needed: an assignment in which we know that God is with us.

I remember calling out to God with similar questions in the most painful times of my life. But God didn't answer my "Why?" God didn't give me what I thought I needed. Instead, God gave me what I really needed—his presence. God let me know that he was still with me. And he held me. And that turned out to be far better than the answers I was seeking. It was all I really needed but didn't know it at the time. But God knew. So Gideon accepts the assignment and trusts that God is with him. This was the first step into leadership.

Conventional wisdom suggests the way to beat an enemy army is to raise a bigger army of your own. So that's what Gideon sets out to do. He rallies the troops. He calls men to arms. He sends out messages to all the tribes to join him in fighting the Midianites. And the people rally and join Gideon. At this point, Gideon has to be feeling pretty good. "Okay, this just might work. The Lord is with me. That angel dude called me a mighty warrior and this new army is getting pretty big. I think we can give the Midianites a run for their money!"

You may have noticed I've used the term *counterintuitive* several times in this chapter. It means something that doesn't make sense and goes against logical thinking, like Seri charging the combine. Well, here comes God throwing a wrench in Gideon's plans with something totally counterintuitive. I can almost hear the conversation between them:

Gideon: "Hey, God, thanks for the anointing and being with me. It really seems to be working. Check out the size of our army! These boys are ready to go! And just look at how many there are."

God: "Yeah, about that. You have too many men in your army."

Gideon: "I'm so excited. We're gonna finally be able to . . . Wait, what?"

God: "You have too many men in your army."

Gideon: "But . . . what do you mean too many? There's no such thing as too many, is there? Don't we want as many as we can get? I know I want as many as we can get. How can we have too many? That just doesn't make sense. I mean, no disrespect, Lord, but this is how it's done. When two armies fight, you want to have the bigger one . . . because that's the one that wins."

God: "You have too many. If I let you win now, your big army will take credit for it."

Gideon: "Okay. . . . Soooo, how small are we talking here?" (cf. Judg 7:1-2).

God eventually whittles Gideon's army down to a mere three hundred warriors. But with this small fraction of an army, God gives Gideon and Israel a great victory and scatters the Midianite army.

The Bible is full of examples like this. Jesus said, "All who want to save their lives will lose them. But all who lose their lives because of me will find them" (Matt 16:25 CEB). "My plans aren't your plans, nor are your ways my ways, says the LORD" (Isa 55:8 CEB).

I Don't Like Boomerangs Anymore

When our two children were small (seven and three years old), we had a two-hour trip in the car. I'm pretty sure I gave the usual parental warning of going to the bathroom before we left. Either they didn't heed my instructions or their little bladders rebelled. Either way, at a most inconvenient time in the journey, the cry rang out in the back seat, "I have to go to the bathroom!" After the obligatory parental questioning of "Why didn't you go before we left?" we realized that we still hadn't solved the immediate pressure building inside our three-year-old son. There was no place to go and no safe place to pull over. I was driving, and my quick-witted wife, Jen, searched desperately and found a plastic ziplock bag previously full of crackers. She held it up with a sly grin.

"What are you going to do with that?" I asked, laughing. She glanced toward our son with an idea forming in her mind. I saw where she was going with this and had my doubts. Being so new out of diapers I doubted the lad had either the inclination or the aim to accomplish her plan. Since I was driving and Jen was bent over into the back seat, I could not see the mechanizations of her scheme in action but after several minutes of struggle, her laugh of glee told me that she had achieved success. Sitting back into her seat, beaming with triumph, she held up the now full ziplock bag. But as she giggled at the daring nature of the whole enterprise, she attempted to complete the project by zipping the bag, which until now remained open and morphing in her hands as she tried to seal the deal—literally. Unbeknownst to Jen before she embarked on this rescue mission, her plastic bag had one major flaw: The ziplock would neither zip nor lock. And this presented us with a very fluid and precarious scenario.

You might not think this would be a time for laughter, but I've found that paroxysms of giggles can strike at the most inopportune time. Now the question presented itself: What to do with this warm bag of liquid sunshine before it spilled all over us. Again, thinking quickly, Jen rolled down her window. I was laughing so hard that I could barely speak my cautionary forebodings of dumping said bag at our current rate of speed. But Jen proceeded, amidst uncontrollable laughter from both the front seat and the back.

To this day I can't explain the mathematics, the aerodynamics, indeed, the very physics of the phenomena that was about to take place. In one fell swoop Jen dumped the contents of the defective bag out the window. And then, somehow, caught in the slipstream of contradictory science, the liquid that spilled out of the car suddenly made a U-turn and boomeranged back through the same window but now at a greater velocity. With this increasing speed added to the liquid, its trajectory bypassed its origin of launch and proceeded to a new destination—the side of the driver's face. The side of my face. At first there was an audible gasp and then seconds of silence as the enormity of this event settled in. I thought for a second my concerned family was sympathizing with me and perhaps even paused in prayer. "Oh, Lord, our patriarch has been struck by boomeranging pee. Please bless him as it drips down the side of his head."

But no such prayer was being uttered. Instead, like the lull before the storm, like the ebb of tide before a tsunami, my family was simply sucking air for an explosion of riotous, uncontrollable "wet your pants if it wasn't already in the bag" laughter. The kind of laughter when you can't get your breath and think you may never stop laughing. They laughed a long time. And I drove on, dripping, trying to figure out things that don't make sense.

Sometimes life and ministry just do not make sense to us. It wasn't logical for Seri to charge the tractor. It didn't make sense to Gideon to fight with only three hundred men. To this day I still do not understand how the flying pee bypassed Jen to hit me in the face! Sometimes we have to do the counterintuitive when we are following Jesus closely. Sometimes we have to charge what scares us. That's called faith.

Questions for Discussion

1. What is a key take-away from this chapter?

2. Have you ever been paralyzed by a fear and unable to make a decision or form a plan?

3. Is your tendency toward fight or flight (charge or run) when confronted by conflict?

4. Has God ever asked you to do something counterintuitive, something that seems like the opposite of what makes the most sense or pragmatic?

5. How can you apply the "Charge What Scares You" principle to your church, family, and workplace?

Chapter 4

THAT'S NOT
YOUR FIGHT

You cannot beat an Arabian horse into submission,
their spirit is too strong.... but this same horse,
treated as an equal, with respect,
love, firm patience, and fairness will want to please you.

—Holly Anderson, Sun Valley Arabians

Insightful people restrain their anger; their glory is to ignore an offense.

—Proverbs 19:11 (CEB)

S eri and I were in the round pen. It had been about a week
since we had ridden together, and she had spent the last
night in her stall. I wanted to let her stretch her legs and
to connect with her before we moved onto the trails.

The round pen, by the way, is a great training tool and has
some interesting lessons for leadership. It's not a complicated tool.
It really is merely a round pen. But the size matters. If it's too big,
you'll spend your time running back and forth. If it's too small,
your horse will crowd you. It needs to be big enough for you to
stand in the middle and connect with your horse as it moves in a
circle around you at the walk, trot, and canter.

The round pen is where a lot of communication and training takes place. As we've learned in previous chapters, the way to communicate with your horse and to teach respect is to move her feet. Horses are very adept at reading body language, and Seri knows what I'm asking by the way I approach her in the round pen. When I want her to move, I give a verbal signal like a *cluck* and then square my shoulders toward her front shoulder in an assertive way. I'm actually "pushing" her with my body posture. She's moving away from my assertive stance. I give a *kiss* sound, and she transitions into the cantor, a controlled run. When I want her to stop, I simply remove the pressure of my squared-up posture and turn sideways to her. Then she immediately stops running and comes to me in the middle of the circle for some loving rubs.

We often spend fifteen to twenty minutes warming up, changing directions frequently and listening to each other in the round pen. Changing directions is important because the round pen isn't just for exercise. It's for learning. Learning to listen and follow instructions in a safe environment. Sometimes, after running for a bit, Seri will ask me if that's enough by lowering her head, licking her lips, and pointing an ear toward me. The round pen is a place for getting to know each other, communicating, learning to take directions, and learning respect.

Whether we are leading horses or people, respect and attention are indispensable. So where is God's "round pen" in your life? It's probably not at a church service. That's too big, and there are too many people around to distract you. More likely, it's in a devotional time where you spend time talking and listening to God. Or in a small group where you are accountable, practicing listening and helping each other. Of course, we need both the public worship service and the private quiet time. We need the big pasture and the round pen to order our lives. The early church did both. "Every day, they met together in the temple and ate in their homes. They shared food with gladness and simplicity" (Acts 2:46 CEB).

There's a sweet rhythm between the large group (in the "temple courts") and the small group (in the homes). As leaders, we need a round pen in our lives—a place where we don't just go to worship, we go to learn from God. The round pen is where we learn to listen, to show respect, and follow instructions. If you don't have that setting right now, I'd suggest you take two steps. One, schedule daily quiet times with God. Consider this your round pen. Spend some time reading scriptures, talking to God, and listening. Two, find a small group or start one with other like-minded Christians.

In the pen with Seri, we were just a few minutes into our usual routine of moving from a walk-trot-cantor, changing directions, backing up, and more. Seri was glad to be out of her stall in the cool morning air. She was going along with the routine when she did something unusual for her. While still running around me in a circle, she looked at me, pinned her ears back, and kicked out at me with her hind legs. She was about ten feet from me so she and I both knew those kicks would not strike close to me. She wasn't trying to hurt me. But she was giving me a message.

To interpret the body language from Seri, here is an analogy most people have encountered. While driving in heavy traffic, a reckless driver changes lanes and cuts in front of you, causing you to slam on brakes. You're frustrated and give a few polite *toots* on your horn, as if to say, "Hey, easy bro! Don't kill anyone today."

But the guy who cut you off doesn't appreciate your polite *toots* or your considerate objection to vehicular homicide. So he flashes you a hand signal that is silent but carries a malicious meaning.

That, my friends, was the message sweet Seri was sending me that day. If she had a middle hoof, she would have displayed it to me. Now, as the leader of the herd, I had a decision to make. How would I respond? Seri's gesture was a clear sign of disrespect. It could even be viewed as a challenge for leadership in our relationship. Consistency is important in all forms of leadership. In working with people and animals you don't want to be the kind of leader who sends mixed signals. As I was trying to decide my next move, another leadership maxim came to mind: "Choose your battles." After a few seconds of mulling it over, I decided how I would respond to Seri's disrespect. I decided to do nothing. I ignored it. I chose to overlook it—at least for the time being. If it kept up, however, I would run her little caboose in that round pen until she found some respect. But for now, my action was to ignore her disrespect.

Don't lose the leadership principle in this decision. Choosing to ignore a problem is not the same as indecision. I chose to "do nothing" as my strategy. Waiting can be an active strategy. With Seri, I chose to temporarily overlook her behavior and act as if I didn't even notice it.

"Insightful people restrain their anger; their glory is to ignore an offense" (Prov 19:11 CEB).

Sometimes the best thing a leader can do is…nothing (see chapter 2). You can't fight every battle. You can't respond to every critic. You can't explain your motives to everyone who misunderstands.

Choose Your Hills Wisely

As a leader, you must choose your battles—and you better choose wisely. If you don't, it can cost you dearly. We're familiar with the military expression "Take the hill." The strategic higher ground must be secured before the troops can advance. Effective generals don't dream vaguely about winning a war. They conceive bite-sized goals that move them to an overall victory. Ground wars are won or lost one inch at a time and one hill at a time. There are often thousands of skirmishes for hills in a single war.

For civilian or church leaders, "the hills" are clear-cut objectives that we lead our people to achieve. It's higher ground that we need to take in order to move our church or organization to the next level. But sometimes leaders have trouble with taking hills. And the trouble generally centers around three predictable complications: We have no hill; we have too many hills; or we choose the wrong hill.

With no hills to take, both the leader and the organization tend to slowly stagnate. The word *plateau* is a familiar concept in organizational leadership. Conversation centers around hills taken in the past, and energy is expended on maintaining the status quo or taking care of members. But in reality, even the status quo tends to move toward decline because leadership is more like riding a bicycle than a mule. You can't just sit still if you want to lead. You have to pedal!

"Where there is no vision, the people perish" (Prov 29:18a KJV).

"When there's no vision, the people get out of control" (Prov 29:18 CEB).

With too many hills to take, the people are busy but not in a unified way. A lot of churches find themselves in this camp. There are programs, events, and meetings, but busyness alone isn't the goal. We need focus, unity, and clarity of vision. We want our efforts to move us somewhere worthwhile.

With the wrong hill, a lot of bad things can happen. You could be completely "successful" at the wrong things. You might have heard the sad declaration of the businessman who spent his entire career climbing the corporate ladder only to realize, "When I got to the top of the ladder I discovered it was leaning against the wrong wall." No matter how successful, if a church isn't pursuing the Great Commandment (loving God and neighbor) and the Great Commission (making disciples), is it really still a church?

Or you could lead your organization into a place it isn't supposed to go. It's a sobering thought. You, a very smart, well-intentioned person, could lead your family, church, or business into disaster. You love God, you pray, you're generous, you keep the commandments... but if you choose the wrong hill or fight a battle that's not yours to fight, it can end in disaster—no matter how well intentioned you are.

If I Could Turn Back Time

I suppose we've all made decisions we wish we could take back. A word spoken in anger, a decision made on impulse. We wish we owned a stainless-steel DeLorean time machine with a fully functioning flux capacitor so we could go back in time and fix it.

But no one probably wishes that more than good King Josiah. Let me remind us of some of his story found in 2 Kings (and retold in 2 Chronicles): "Josiah was eight years old when he became king, and he ruled for thirty-one years in Jerusalem.... He did what was right in the LORD's eyes, and walked in the ways of his ancestor David—not deviating from it even a bit to the right or left" (2 Kgs 22:1-2 CEB).

And that's saying something, because Josiah had a crummy example to follow. The scriptural text refers to Josiah following his "father David," but that's reaching back in time a bit to his ancestor David. His birthfather, King Amon, was a complete failure at following God, and his grandfather, King Manasseh, is credited with turning the nation of Judah away from God to worshipping idols in the temple! If Josiah sent a DNA sample to myroyalheritage.com it would come back with a genealogy like this:

"Grandfather Manasseh"—evil, known murderer, sacrificed one of his sons by fire to a pagan god, caused the nation to turn away from God;

"Father Amon"—evil, followed in footsteps of his father, assassinated by his staff.

Enter Josiah at eight years old. Imagine being told, "We just killed your dad, but we're making you the new king. We'll be running things until you are an adult—and watching to see if the family evil streak is genetic. Remember, we don't have elections; we have swords."

It looks like the poor child doesn't have a chance to be anything more than his heritage: a selfish, evil monarch who only cares about his own wealth and preservation.

But something remarkable happens. Josiah breaks the pattern. Through the influence of a godly priest, he becomes a good king. So good that he destroys the idol worship established by his father and grandfather and returns the whole nation to following

God. Things had gotten so corrupt under his predecessors that they had even misplaced the Torah, the Instruction Scroll, which is probably our book of Deuteronomy (which means "the second law")! During renovation, it's found encased in the temple wall, and Josiah declares that God's people should read this Instruction and do what it says (2 Kgs 22)!

Josiah repairs God's temple, destroys idols that substitute for the LORD, reestablishes Passover (2 Kgs 23), and leads the people to turn back faithfully to God! He follows God so thoroughly and loyally he's compared to the Israel's greatest king, David. You would almost think, unlike David, that this king could do no wrong.

But that's not the case. Even though he loved God, even though he was obedient, even though he led his nation away from idols and back to God, he still made a tragic mistake that cost him his life. He picked the wrong hill. He fought a battle that wasn't his to fight.

Here's the story from 2 Chronicles 35:

Things are good in the kingdom, much better than they've been in years. The homicide rate is down because the king is not murdering people. Folks aren't sacrificing their children by fire anymore. The temple has been restored, and the economy is really going well. Good King Josiah is way up in the popularity polls and even being lauded as the best king ever.

And that's when Egypt's King Neco comes knocking. Neco has an army with him, but he's not attacking Josiah. He's passing through a neighboring region on his way to Carchemish to fight some upstarts called the Babylonians, who seem to have world domination among their ambitions.

Josiah decides to gather his army and fight King Neco. We are not told Josiah's motivation. Perhaps he wondered which world power would be more dangerous. Perhaps he wondered, "What would King David do? He fought Goliath; I think I'll go fight Neco." And so he marches out to fight. But King Neco tries to make peace. He sends ambassadors to Josiah with these words:

"What do you want with me, king of Judah?" he asked. "I haven't come to attack you today. I'm after the dynasty that wars with me. God told me to hurry, and he is on my side. Get out of God's way, or he will destroy you." But Josiah wouldn't turn back. Instead, he camouflaged himself in preparation for battle, refusing to listen to Neco's words from God's own mouth, and went to fight Neco on the plain of Megiddo (2 Chr 35:21-22 CEB).

From the story in 2 Kings, we know Josiah is a good man and a good king. He loves God. He's done tremendous good, pursuing righteousness and justice for the nation. But he refuses to turn back. Was it pride? Did he feel he would lose credibility if, after all the trouble of marching out the army, he were to turn back now? Did he fear Babylon more than Egypt? Did he think "Hey, God is with me, not with you"? He doesn't realize he is about to attack the wrong hill.

Josiah attacks and is hit by one of Neco's archers. He retreats from the battle but dies from his wounds. Everyone mourns the loss of their good king. Jeremiah the prophet writes funeral songs to honor Josiah. Choirs sing. People cry. All the pomp and circumstance of a royal funeral is arranged to honor this great man in death. But a royal funeral is still a funeral.

Josiah's lesson is a bit uncomfortable for us.

You can love God. You can be obedient. You can seek righteousness. You can do great things for your family, your church, and even your nation. And you can still suffer catastrophe and even death if you choose the wrong hill to take and try to fight a battle that's not yours to fight.

As a leader, that makes me say, "Yikes!"

So, how do we avoid choosing the wrong hill and fighting the wrong battle? Hills and battles can sometimes look pretty similar from our vantage point. Here are some scriptures to guide us:

1. *Communicate.* Jesus says, "I can't do anything by myself. Whatever I hear, I judge, and my judgment is just. I don't seek my own will but the will of the one who sent me" (John 5:30 CEB). *Stay close to God.* I think Jesus would tell us that staying close to God is not only important but essential. Imagine a military captain on the battlefield as a spiritual metaphor. He has studied maps and strategies and philosophies and theories of battle. But how does he know which hill to take? Communication with his Superior Officer.

2. *Don't put all your trust in your feelings or intelligence.* "Trust in the LORD with all your heart; don't rely on your own intelligence. Know him in all your paths, and he will keep your ways straight" (Prov 3:5-6 CEB).

3. *Get good advice.* "Without guidance, a people will fall, but there is victory with many counselors" (Prov 11:14 CEB).

4. *Pray this prayer:* "Lord, please protect us; especially from ourselves." This prayer is not magical or foolproof, but this is a prayer we pray around our church. If prayed sincerely, it will have great effect. Note that this prayer embodies the first and second suggestions above.

By the way, in case you're wondering how Seri's sassy attitude turned out in the round pen, it simply worked itself out. After I ignord her kicking out at me, she did a few more laps, got it out of her system, and eased back into her normal self. Everyone can have a grumpy day—even horses. Just remember: When dealing with grumpy people or grumpy horses, pick your battles wisely.

Questions for Discussion

1. Where is God's "round pen" in your life? Where do you go to listen and learn privately and intimately? What can you do to spend more time as a learner in God's round pen?

2. What trouble have you experienced in taking hills? Have you tended to take no hills, too many hills, or the wrong hills?

3. What would it look like to take the next hill for your church? Marriage? Family? Faith? Business? Other?

4. Consider praying the "prayer of protection" on behalf of your church, family, business, or country: "Lord, please protect us, especially from ourselves.

5. Have you ever felt too busy to reach your actual goal? How can you stop getting in your own way?

6. What battles are you facing now? Which do you need to ignore because they aren't worth fighting? Which do you need to ignore because it's not your fight? Which battles do you need to charge head on?

Chapter 5

LEADERS AND NEW IDEAS

Your frustration begins where your knowledge ends.

—Clinton Anderson

All leaders are learners.

—Rick Warren

No one sews a piece of new, unshrunk cloth on old clothes because the patch tears away the cloth and makes a worse tear. No one pours new wine into old wineskins. If they did, the wineskins would burst, the wine would spill, and the wineskins would be ruined. Instead, people pour new wine into new wineskins so that both are kept safe.

—Matthew 9:16-17 (CEB)

I enjoy reading novels, especially historical fiction. This is where an author takes an actual historical event but tells the story from a fictional character's point of view. Good writers in this genre help us learn something about history while we are being drawn into a well-told story. One of my favorite authors in this style is Wilbur Smith. Most of Smith's novels take place in Africa, and he has a series of books that are filled with details from historical events in ancient Egypt. This is where our subject matter merges with Mr. Smith's novels—horses, leaders, and the acceptance or rejection of new innovations.

We generally think horses have been around since the dawn of human experience. But what many don't realize is that horses haven't been around *everywhere* since the dawn of time. In his novel *River God*,[1] Smith describes how the Hyksos people conquered Egypt through the use of a new and unheard of technology—the horse.

The Hyksos were a Semitic people originally from Syria and Palestine and living in the Egyptian Delta, which is between the modern nations of Israel and Egypt. The Hyksos did not invent warfare using horses and chariots, but they improved and introduced those weapons when they rose up to overthrow the current Egyptian rulers. In warfare, they improved the horse and chariot, which had been invented around 2000 BC. They employed the composite bow, and they used battle-axes made of bronze.[2]

Around 1650 BC no one in Egypt knows much about the Hyksos people; they heard only rumors about their names and their origins to the north among other outcast tribes. Their nickname of "shepherd kings" (Hyksos) comes from a Greek historian who lived around 300 BC. In Egyptian, their name means "ruler of foreign lands." The Egyptians (at least in their own estimations) were the most advanced people in culture, learning, technology and warfare in the known world. But oftentimes the "known world" is smaller than we think and is always changing.

---

1. Wilbur Smith, *River God* (New York: St. Martin's Press, 1994).
2. See https://www.britannica.com/topic/Hyksos-Egyptian-dynasty and the New Interpreter's Dictionary of the Bible entry on the Hyksos.

Rumors were surfacing frequently about these outcasts and immigrants until the Egyptian leaders could not ignore them any longer. It seems these mysterious Hyksos were somehow conquering tribes and kingdoms and moving closer to the center of Egyptian power at an unheard rate of speed. The novelist Wilbur Smith imagines an invasion this way:

> From the front ranks of the Hyksos formations some of these strange vehicles started towards us. A murmur went up from our ranks as we saw how fast they were moving. The range closed and another cry went up from our host as we realized that these vehicles were each being drawn by a pair of extraordinary beasts.
>
> They stood as tall as the wild Oryx, with the same stiff, upstanding mane along the crest of their arched necks. They were not horned like the Oryx, but their heads were more gracefully formed. Their eyes were large and their nostrils flared. Their legs were long and hoofed. Striding out with a peculiar daintiness, they seemed merely to brush the surface of the desert.
>
> Even now after all these years, I can recapture the thrill of gazing at a horse for the first time. In my mind the beauty of the hunting cheetah paled beside these marvelous beasts. At the same time we were filled with fear of them, and I heard one of the officers near me cry out, "Surely these monsters are killers, and eaters of human flesh!"
>
> A stirring horror ran through our formations, as we expected these beasts to fall upon us and devour us like ravening lions. But the leading vehicle swung away and sped parallel to our front rank. It moved on spinning discs, and I stared at it in wonder. For the first few moments I was so stunned by what I was looking at that my mind refused to absorb it all. If anything, my first sight of a chariot was almost as moving as the horses that drew it.[3]

And it happened. The most advanced civilization in the known world was overthrown by an upstart bunch of barbarians who possessed unexpected technology and new strategies. The

---

3. Wilbur Smith, *River God* (New York: St. Martin's Press, 1994), 378-79.

Egyptians reacted to the horse, chariot, and wheel with a pattern that hasn't changed much through the millennia—with fear, resistance, and a stubborn lack of acknowledgment about the threat.

You can almost hear the old politicians debate. "Our sledges have worked fine for thousands of years, and I see no reason why we should abandon what's worked for us so long for some new-fangled, fly-by-night invention called the wheel. I'd rather see our Egypt die and me in it, than to abandon the way of life our ancestors taught us."

And they did... die that is. They were defeated because they were behind in the latest technology of the day. They lost their kingdom and many lost their lives because they either couldn't see the need to adapt, didn't know how to adapt, or refused to adapt.

Because change doesn't have manners and rarely knocks. Instead, it comes barreling in, giving us little time to react. And if we stand in its path long enough trying to decide what to do, we are run over by the wheels of change. Leaders need to be ready to deal with change.

> Change is coming but many:
> don't see the need to adapt;
> don't know how to adapt; or
> refuse to adapt.

Just ask the taxi industry or movie rental stores. Actually, you probably can't find a movie rental store to ask, but that's my point. In a previous book about small-group ministries, *Grab, Gather, Grow: Multiply Community Groups in Your Church* my wife, Jen, and I list seven key insights from an essay by church consultant Carey Nieuwhof regarding the rise of Uber and the response of the traditional taxi industry. His analogy and observations are especially pertinent for church leaders:

1. Owning a great taxi cab is no longer enough.
2. Innovation doesn't ask for approval.
3. Fighting change doesn't stop change.
4. When you confuse method with mission, you lose.
5. Your past success is no guarantee of your future success.
6. Innovation spawns more innovation, while defensiveness spawns death.
7. Self-interest will inevitably lose to public interest.[4]

With the rise of Uber, there have been angry protests, petitions, and lawsuits by the taxi industry and by drivers. But many taxicabs have gone out of business. I've often wondered why local taxi companies didn't develop their own app, make calling a cab as easy as Uber, or lower their prices to be competitive. As they say, "Hindsight is 20/20." It's much harder to see ahead and even harder to know what to do about the wheels of change rolling your way.

The Old Egyptians could have used these lessons in 1650 BC when they faced the Hyksos uprising. They were confronted with technology and an enemy that they could not understand. And they either couldn't or wouldn't adapt in a timely way. They lost their kingdom and way of life, the very things they were trying to preserve.

These lessons from history and lessons from the business world should make churches take notice of disruption too, because

---

4. Jennifer and Jim Cowart, *Grab, Gather, Grow: Multiply Community Groups in Your Church* (Nashville: Abingdon Press, 2016), 1–5.

change is rolling through our culture at a rapid pace, whether we like it or not. And as leaders we must learn to adapt to flourish—or even survive.

Now, before you get up in arms about me trying to change your church, let me clarify a bit. There is a huge difference between *mission* and *methods*. The mission of the church doesn't change. In fact, we can't change the mission of the church because it's not our church. It's God's. And God's mission, communicated through the life of Jesus, is fully contained in two summary statements we label as the Great Commandment (love God and love your neighbor) and the Great Commission (make disciples) to keep us on task. The church must always be faithful to the Great Commandment and the Great Commission. We can't vote on it. We don't need a meeting to revise it. The mission is set.

But methods are different. Methods need to change. In fact, they must change in order to carry out the mission among new generations. Methods don't have the same status as mission. Methods, the way we do things, are similar to new technologies and new strategies.

If the church doesn't see the need to adapt our methods, doesn't know how to adapt our methods, or refuses to adapt our methods, then a chasm will appear between a church and its culture, and it will be run over by change. It will become ineffective in completing our mission.

Leaders need to adapt to change.

Pastor Andy Stanley[5] offers several helpful suggestions for leaders to navigate change:

5. Andy Stanley presented these suggestions for leaders at the 2017 Global Leadership Summit. He is founder of North Point Ministries, which began as a col-

1. *Be a student of change.* Recognize that we have a natural tendency to resist things we don't understand and can't control. If we are aware, then we can do something about it. Also, be humble enough to learn from the generations coming behind us. Listen to the college students, high-school students, and middle-schoolers. They may not have the answers, but they can often see some of the problems with old methods! And they'll tell you if you ask them sincerely.

2. *Listen to outsiders.* Listen to people not in the church world. After all, that's who we're trying to reach.

3. *Replace "how" with "wow."* I've tried to do this with my staff. Here's how it works: Ask for fresh new ideas, and when your staff or volunteers bring them start by saying, "wow." "Wow" helps generate creativity and discussion. "How" tends to shut down creativity and put the idea-giver on the defensive. You won't use every idea, but if you value the creative effort with an affirming "wow," chances are you will foster a healthier, more creative environment.

Let's pause here for a brief leadership self-evaluation: How do you handle change? Are you open to new ideas, new methods, and new technology? I'm not quick to answer "Yes," but I'm working on it. And, I think it's a little harder now than when I was younger.

When we started a new congregation in 2001 in southern Georgia, we were considered an *innovation*. We were the first in our area to use technology, play contemporary music, and use skits and testimonies as part of the message. That doesn't sound very innovative

laborative of six churches in the Atlanta area. Recently, *Outreach Magazine* identified Stanley as one of the Top 10 Most Influential Pastors in America.

now; tens of thousands of churches do this. But when we first started among a sea of churches with very formal services, wearing robes and playing organ music, we stuck out as being new and unique. But here's the point: We're not new *anymore*. Innovation has a shelf life. So, now as a maturing organization, we face the challenge of change—how to balance two sometimes opposing elements, holding onto the core values that must never change, while at the same time being open, flexible, and innovative with our methods.

Danger is imminent when leaders migrate to one of two extremes about change, and either can throw a church out of balance. Some leaders tend to chase whatever new fad comes along. If social media is touting it, and other churches are trying it, they jump on board. But on the other end of the spectrum, some leaders would rather die than change anything. In their view, to change seems like disloyalty to people or systems or traditions that they feel called to preserve. Both of these extremes are out of balance.

In Matthew 9:17, Jesus talks about wine and wineskins. Glass bottles weren't available in the ancient Near East, so goatskins were cleaned and sewn together to make drinking and storage bags. "Hey, could you pass the dead goat? I'm thirsty."

As the fermentation process transformed grape juice to wine, there was expansion that stretched the bags. Old, tough skins, as you can imagine, are not pliable like new, fresh skins. So you don't put "new wine," which is still expanding as it ages, into old, inflexible skins. If you do, it's a huge mess waiting to happen. The new wine will eventually burst the old skin, spilling the wine, ruining the skin, and making a stain on the white camel hair mat that will never come out.

Look at this passage again: "No one pours new wine into old wineskins. If they did, the wineskins would burst, the wine would spill, and the wineskins would be ruined. Instead, people pour new wine into new wineskins so that both are kept safe" (Matt 9:17 CEB).

Jesus didn't come to "patch up," improve, or fix the old religious system (the old wineskin). Instead, he came to establish a new covenant (requiring a new wineskin) through his sacrificial death. Perhaps that's why Jesus didn't invite Pharisees or legal experts to the inner circle among his first disciples. They were likely too ingrained in the tradition to accept something new.

The Pharisees, Sadducees, and legal experts (scribes) were part of the old guard. They loved the Law. Their habits and practices depended on the Law. Like the Egyptians watching the approach of chariots, they refused to let go of old methods to embrace the new. And when they saw and heard Jesus, most reacted with fearful defensiveness.

Jesus didn't throw out the old covenant, which is based on the evergreen mission to love God and neighbor. He fulfilled the Law in a new way: "Don't even begin to think that I have come to do away with the Law and the Prophets. I haven't come to do away with them but to fulfill them" (Matt 5:17 CEB).

The sum of all the commandments—the mission to love God and neighbor (Deut 6:5 and Lev 19:18)—never changes. But Jesus comes with an additional "co"-mission that never changes and further fulfills or implements the Great Commandment. We are faithful to Jesus's mission by baptizing and make disciples among all tribes and nations (Matt 19).

Even as you remain faithful to God's mission for the church, it is possible for change to overwhelm your vision and stamina. Like a horse, you can be run right into the ground. Find a healthy balance and pace. Don't fear change. But don't chase too hard after it either. It would be foolish to conclude that "old = bad" and "new = good." That polarization is just not the case with tradition or innovation. Sometimes the old ways are better. But the old methods often must be updated to keep moving toward the age-old mission.

Questions for Discussion:

1. Is change exciting or uncomfortable to you?

2. Has the fear of change ever prevented your progress?

3. Does your church need to adapt to any changes right now? What would this change look like for your area and congregation?

4. How can you improve your methods without compromising your mission?

5. Think of a specific recent idea for which you and your leaders could encourage creativity by saying "wow" instead of "how."

6. How can you get better at handling change?

7. What things in your life, church, and home need to change?

Chapter 6

CHASE BUTTERFLIES
AND ELEPHANTS
THE SAME

*If you are fond of a horse and wish to do him a real favor—train him
well. Teach him good manners, good habits both in the stable and
under saddle. You need never worry about the future of such a horse
if for any reason you may have to part with him. You assure him
of friends wherever he goes. Perhaps the greatest kindness you can
do any horse is to educate him well.*

—Tom Roberts

*Whoever is faithful with little is also faithful with much,
and the one who is dishonest with little is also dishonest with much.*

—Luke 16:10 (CEB)

A few years ago, Jen, our daughter Aly, and I traveled to
Africa with Compassion International to learn more
about their ministry. We visited Uganda and Kenya
and saw the good work this ministry is doing with child sponsor-
ship and more. Since then, our church members have collectively
partnered with Compassion International, to sponsor over eight

67

hundred children around the world! It's a great partnership and worth looking into.[1]

As a leader, taking care of poor and defenseless people is one of the things on our "To-Do list" from Jesus. In Matthew 25:31-46, Jesus gives a list of the actions we either do or don't do in his name: food for the hungry, drink for the thirsty, shelter for the stranger, clothing for the naked, and care for the sick and those in prison. He then uses two metaphors based on our action or inaction. The folks who "DO" are called sheep. And the folks who "DON'T" are called goats. Believe me, we want to be sheep. In Jesus's story of the sheep and goats, good intentions and well-meaning thoughts don't count. It's our actions that put us on his right side or left side.

At the end of our tour of the ministry sites, we had the opportunity to go on a safari. This was a dream come true because I'm a National Geographic/Discovery channel kind of guy. As a kid, I loved Tarzan movies and learned to love the animals of Africa from afar—and now the chance to see them up close with my wife and daughter was incredible. As our little bush plane approached the landing strip in the Masai Mara, we saw zebra and antelope scurrying out of the way. From a few seats behind us, Aly shouted, "Dad, I just saw a lion!"

Africa boasts of "the Big Five," some of the largest and most dangerous animals in the world. They are the elephant, lion, cape buffalo, rhino, and leopard. What's the most dangerous? You might be surprised because it's not included in the five. The most dangerous creature in Africa is the mosquito, and it is responsible

---

1. If you or your church are looking for a strategic partner in helping relieve human suffering, consider the work of Compassion Internation, www.compassion.com.

for killing more people than any other by carrying diseases such as malaria.

On our little safari, we were able to see four of the Big Five, but the elusive leopard could not be found on our trip. It was a great adventure to see these wild animals up close. My only disappointment was that our son Josh and Seri weren't with us! Ha. Josh has since made it to Africa, but Seri has yet to make the trip. They just don't serve hay on Delta flights, so she's staying home.

But oh, what fun it would be to ride with her on safari! How I've dreamed of galloping on her back, keeping stride with the wildebeest migration and chasing zebra across the plains.

When I got back home, that dream of galloping across the African wildlands didn't leave me, so I began to do a little research about hunters in Africa from the 1800s who traveled and hunted from horseback. One favorite is a gentleman named F. C. Selous. He was a contemporary of and friends with President Teddy Roosevelt. In fact, Mr. Roosevelt, along with others, called Selous the greatest African hunter of all time.

Now, I realize in our day of political correctness regarding hunting, I may have lost some of you here. If so, you may want to skip this chapter. I love the outdoors and hunting, but I don't feel a need to try to convert you to my passions in this area, nor do I wish you to try to convert me away from them. But if you can stick with me past the hunting story, I think you will glean an important lesson about leadership.

Mr. Selous lived in a different era than ours, which is overcrowded, over-fished, and over-hunted in many parts of the world. He made his living by hunting elephants and other wild game before they were endangered. The writer tells his stories in a very humble, almost matter-of-fact way. Here is one excerpt of a particularly dicey experience he had while hunting elephants. The elephant he is pursuing is wounded, his horse exhausted from the chase, and now Selous is confronted with an angry elephant who is about to turn the tables. The hunter becomes the hunted.

> Digging the spurs into my horse's ribs, I did my best to get him away, but he was so thoroughly done that, instead of springing forwards, which was what the emergency required, he only started at a walk, and was just breaking into a canter, when the elephant was upon us. I heard two short sharp screams above my head, and had just time to think it was all over for me, when, horse and all, I was dashed to the ground. For a few seconds I was half-stunned by the violence of the shock, and the first thing I became aware of, was a very strong smell of elephant. At the same instant I felt that I was not much hurt, and that, though in an unpleasant predicament, I had still a chance for life.... At last with a violent effort I wrenched myself loose, and threw my body over sideways, so that I rested on my hands. As I did so I saw the hind-legs of the elephant standing like two pillars before me, and at once grasped the situation. She was on her knees, with her head and tusks in the ground, and I had been pressed down under her chest, but luckily behind her forelegs. Dragging myself from under her, I regained my feet and made a hasty retreat, having had rather enough of elephants for the time being.[2]

Wow, what an account! But also given in his typical way. Selous is very British and reserved, and I think that's one of the things that makes him so likeable.

Q: "How was your day, Mr. Selous?"

A: "Oh, splendid, just splendid, my boy. Thanks for asking. Beautiful morning, don't you know."

Q: "Any adventures today?"

---

2. Frederick Courtney Selous, *A Hunter's Wanderings in Africa* (London: Macmillan, 1907; reprinted 2009), 365.

A: "No, not really. Though I did have a bit of a sticky wicket with an elephant, what? Not much to speak of though. Still kicking, as you can see. Now, how about a spot of tea, old boy? I'm simply famished."

I know elephants are dangerous. They don't roam the neighborhood where I live, but one of my dear friends, Dr. Michael Lowerikoi from the Maasai tribe in Kenya, lost his father in an elephant attack. So to hear Selous describe his brush with death by crushing as an "unpleasant predicament" is quite the understatement! But that's the kind of man Selous was. He faced charges by lions and buffalo with the same calm reserve. Never claiming to be fearless, only trying to demonstrate courage through the fear in the face of danger.

But Mr. Selous was no cold-hearted killer. In fact, he loved nature and was a distinguished naturalist and conservationist. And here's one of the things that caught my attention about Selous and inspired this chapter. When he wasn't hunting elephants, he was chasing butterflies. Literally. He was a very serious *lepidopterist*. Yes, I had to look it up too, but it's the name of a scientist who studies butterflies and moths.

So picture this. One day he's riding his gallant steed into the hunt. His heart is racing. He knows his quarry is out there. He gallops over the savannah looking for signs of his potential game. He has his trusty rifle and his faithful horse and they are on the hunt for elephants.

Then, the next day. He rides his gallant steed into the hunt. His heart is racing. He knows his quarry is out there. He gallops over the savannah looking for signs of his potential game. He has his trusty butterfly net and his faithful horse and they are on the hunt for butterflies.

Selous stalked, loved, and hunted the elephant and the butterfly the same. Same passion. Same zeal. Same preparation. Same thrill of the hunt. And that's impressive. Listen to his enthusiasm:

> Why I feel the absence of the sun so acutely is because, when the sun is not shining, no butterflies...are to be got...for you can't think how I put my whole soul into egg and butterfly collecting when I'm at it...but it is hopeless work collecting butterflies in bad weather. I think I must be set down as a harmless lunatic by the peasants in the neighborhood already.[3]

I love this guy's passion! As I thought of his exploits, it suddenly dawned on me, "Jim, you can't hunt elephants on horseback, but you can hunt butterflies!" So how do you hunt butterflies on horseback? I didn't know, but I was determined to give it a try.

First, I needed the right equipment, so I set off for one of my favorite outdoor stores. Now, unlike Jen, I'm not much of a shopper. Unless it's at a sporting goods store. I can wander for hours looking at guns and knives and fishing gear. I'd been to this particular store many times but never for the equipment I was looking for today. Actually, I felt a bit sheepish walking down the aisles of hunting equipment. I wondered if I'd get a snicker from some of the hunters in the store if they knew I was looking for butterfly equipment. And then I remembered Selous. He faced charging elephants, lions, and buffalo, and he chased butterflies. So I swallowed my pride and tried to make my voice sound confident and a little deeper as I asked a salesperson, "Ummm, excuse me. Do you have any butterfly nets?"

"Why yes, sir, we do. That will be in the children's department."

3. John Guille Millais, *Life of Frederick Courtney Selous* (reprint from 1918 ed. by Gallery Pub., 2006), 52.

"Oh brother."

"What's that, sir?"

"Never mind."

I bought three butterfly nets, a small butterfly holder to attach to my saddle, and a bigger habitat to keep butterflies in. I was so excited! Immediately I set out for the butterfly hunting grounds. I had noticed that on one of the properties where I ride there were a lot of wildflowers and therefore a lot of butterflies, so I picked up Seri and headed to the woods.

Ridiculous reenactment of a butterfly hunt!

I'm sure if you could have seen me that day you would have laughed. I was even laughing at myself. I saddled up, attached the container to the saddle, grabbed my biggest net and set off. Seri didn't know what we were doing! But "everything is training!" I love to expose Seri to different scenarios and activities. I've played frisbee and tennis on Seri as well as tried mounted archery, shooting arrows at targets. The more things I expose her to, the more things she experiences, she understands there is less to fear and she trusts and listens to me more. Actually, I think this is what God does with us too. Exposes us to situations that we are uncomfortable with so we learn to listen and trust him more.

Now, let me ask you a question. When is the last time you've chased a butterfly? I mean, you went all out to catch one? For me,

I suppose it had not been attempted since childhood. And now here I was, fully equipped, on a horse, looking for butterflies. No, let me correct that. I wasn't looking. I was *hunting!* Just like the elephant hunter Selous. If, like me, it's been a while since you chased a butterfly, let me remind you that they are downright fast! Even faster than a horse I found out. At least quicker with their bobbing and weaving. I was laughing so hard, Seri must have thought I was crazy by the way I was bobbing and weaving trying to follow their fluttering path. It brought to mind the boxer Muhammad Ali, who boasted that he could "float like a butterfly and sting like a bee."

After many unsuccessful attempts of chasing them through the fields, taking wild and fruitless swipes with my net, I decided it was time to change tactics. And that's when I developed my own version of the "butterfly stalk." Here's how it goes. I ride along looking for both blooming flowers and butterflies. When I spot my quarry, I slow Seri to a walk, and we move stealthily forward to within about ten yards. Then, with heart pounding, I slip from Seri and begin my final stalk. I creep forward, sometimes on hands and knees until I am within striking distance. I wait for the butterfly to settle...and then...I pounce! And I have to tell you, I get it. I get the thrill that Selous must have felt from the hunt, whether he was stalking elephant or butterflies. I've made a few successful captures from horseback, but most of my success has been from the stalk. I then put the butterflies into my portable container attached to the saddle. When we finish for the day, I transfer our game into the larger habitat, enjoy them for a few days and then release them, no worse for wear.

So, you may be wondering what all this has to do with leadership. Fair question. Let me see if I can connect the leadership dots for us. Selous hunted elephants and butterflies the same way. One is huge and one is small. But he pursued the large and the small with the same passion and enthusiasm. That's a good lesson for us leaders.

Some people want to be great leaders or successful or wealthy. They are waiting for their "big break." They want to make the big play in the game, preach to a huge crowd, close the big deal, or rush in and be the hero with spotlights and applause. They want the elephant, but tend to think the butterfly is beneath them. As a pastor, sometimes people tell me they will start tithing when they get more money. And I think, *No, you won't. Because if you're not faithful with a little, you're not going to be faithful with a lot.*

Do you know the old joke about tithing?

A young businessman goes to his pastor and asks him to pray for a new business venture he is starting. "I'm going to be faithful from the start and tithe from whatever profit God gives," the young man enthuses. The pastor prays for the young man and his business, "Lord, I believe this young man is sincere. Please help him be successful and keep you first."

A few years later, the same not-so-young man sets up an appointment with the pastor. "I've got a problem and need to talk with you," he says. The man explains that his business has been a huge success, but that's the problem. "When I began, ten percent of the profits seemed reasonable. But now that the business has grown, well, ten percent of that just seems like an exorbitant amount to give." The pastor nods with kind eyes and says, "I understand completely. Let me pray for you again." The businessman sighs with relief until the pastor starts praying.

"Lord, thank you for answering our prayer and making this young man's business so successful. However, he makes so much money now that his tithe back to you is just too big for him to feel comfortable with. Would you please reduce his profits down to a place where he'll feel more comfortable tithing again? Amen." Ha!

No one begins with elephants. Not even Selous. As a boy he chased butterflies around his native England. But he never outgrew them either. He never thought they were beneath his best efforts even after moving to bigger game.

Jesus puts forth a principle about generosity, stewardship, and leadership. "If you are faithful in little things, you will be faithful in large ones. But if you are dishonest in little things, you won't be honest with greater responsibilities" (Luke 16:10 NLT).

So as leaders, lets do whatever task is before us with zeal and passion. What's the biggest and most important thing you do? Perhaps that's your elephant. Now, what's the smallest most mundane of your responsibilities? Perhaps that's your butterfly. Do both jobs the same! Toilet overflows? Jump in there and clean it up with passion. Working on a ten million dollar project or a ten dollar project, do them both the same.

Many times we are in "Gods School" and we don't even realize it. For example, David faced the lion and the bear, both formidable opponents. "'The LORD,' David added, 'who rescued me from the power of both lions and bears, will rescue me from the power of this Philistine'" (1 Sam 17:37 CEB).

But these battles were really just "classes" for facing Goliath. If he hadn't trusted God and done well with the lion and bear, he wouldn't have been ready for Goliath.

"Lions 101 . . . A+"

"Bears 201 . . . A+ Excellent!"

"I believe the lad is ready for Giants 301. If he'll just apply the lessons he's learned from 101 and 201, he should be able to handle 301 just fine."

If you aren't a good steward with a thousand dollars, why would God give you a million dollars? You'll just kill yourself with it! And he cares more about your soul than your comfort!

Protecting the orphans from a charging bear. (Just kidding.)

Remember the story Jesus tells about the sheep and the goats. The actions were so small in the scheme of things that both groups asked, "When?"

"When did we see you hungry and feed you, Lord?"

"When did we see you hungry and *not* feed you, Lord?"

But Jesus isn't talking about feeding him literally. He says that when we DO or DON'T to the "least of these, my brothers," then we've done it to him. It's in the little actions for the "least of these" that makes all the difference.

Some leaders are always dreaming of the next big thing. Dreaming is good. But not if you are dreaming so much that you're doing a crummy job with the task before you. A pastor once told me that the church he was serving was a good

Seri tip toes in the butterfly stalk.

"stepping-stone" for his future. That's insulting to the people he was pastoring.

There are certainly leaders throughout history who have not followed these principles. But we don't want to just be great leaders. We want to be leaders worth following. Let's be like Selous. Let's hunt our elephants and our butterflies the same way.

Questions for Discussion

1. How well do you accomplish the "little assignments" that aren't glamorous or get much attention?

2. "God doesn't waste anything." How does this statement connect the little things in ministry with the big things? When's the last time you tried something new, like chasing butterflies?

3. Do you think David would have been able to challenge Goliath without his experiencewith the lion and bear? Why or why not?

4. Read again Jesus's teaching about the sheep and the goats in Matthew 25:31-46. Have you ever thought about this as a "To-Do List" from Jesus? How are you doing with this assignment? How is your church doing?

Chapter 7

WHEN LEADERS GET LOST

Ain't nothing like riding a fine horse in new country.

—*Augustus McCrae,* Lonesome Dove

*I have never been lost, but I will admit to being confused
for a couple of weeks.*

—*Daniel Boone*

For the Son of Man came to seek and to save the lost.

—*Luke 19:10 (NIV)*

I love to load Seri on the trailer and head out to explore new trails or dirt roads. There's just something about seeing new territory that is exciting to me. So I'm always on the lookout for new places to explore. Not too long ago, a friend told me about some riding trails called "1099" in a national forest about an hour from home. I still don't know why it's called 1099, and the directions to get there were almost as mysterious as the name. I was told there are no signs to mark the entrance, and I was only given what I call "country directions." You're gonna need to go about thirty to forty miles east. Then take a right at that gas station, the one that

79

sells the good biscuits.... Actually I'm not sure it's still there. But they sure had some good biscuits. Go on past where Wilson's barn burned down and turn left. If you get to a bunch of cows, you've gone too far. You get the idea. So we loaded up and headed out, and to my surprise, we actually found it. And it was beautiful! Great trails that meandered through old-growth forest and next to a beautiful river. It was definitely worth the drive and search. Since then Seri and I have made that trip many times.

On about our third ride there, we were heading back to the trailer after a full day of exploring. We had covered a lot of miles, played in the river, gotten turned around a time or two, and all in all enjoyed a great ride. We hadn't seen another person all day, so I was surprised to meet an older couple on horseback coming from the opposite direction about the same time we arrived back at my truck. We exchanged greetings, complimented each other's horses, and asked about each other's ride. After a few minutes of small talk, they asked me a question that took me by surprise. "These are some really nice trails, but have you ever ridden 1099?" I sputtered for a few seconds with my laughter and said, "That's where I thought I was right now!" "No," they explained, "that's a few miles back."

Evidently, I wasn't where I thought I was.

Because sometimes you're lost and don't know it.

Have you ever been lost? Most of us have. It can be an unsettling experience. Maybe that's putting it too mildly. It can actually be downright terrifying. Panic is not our friend. It grows inside us like a monster choking our speech and fogging our thinking.

I remember as a kid going to Six Flags in Atlanta for the first time. I was so excited. There were a lot of "firsts" for me that day. First time in the big city. First time to an amusement park.

And first time being lost. My parents were on the trip as chaper-
ones, and I'm sure my mom must have said "stay close to us" a
dozen times. And I meant to…but I wandered off. I don't know

Working the cows. Everything is training.

how long it took, but after a while I glanced around the hustle and
bustle of humanity and noticed, "Hey, I don't know any of these
people." Only I didn't think it that clearly or calmly. I felt panic
swell up in my stomach and race through my body. I couldn't
think and I couldn't talk and I felt tears cloud my vision, threatening to pour out in front of all these strangers.

And then I did the worst thing you can do when you are lost.
I ran. I just started running blindly, driven by the panic. It was like
in a Disney movie when you're running through the forest and
suddenly the friendly looking trees turn into monsters and start
reaching out for you with their branches. I ran without purpose
or direction, zigzagging around the park. And the more I ran, the
more lost I became, and the panic never let up. Eventually I had to
stop running from pure exhaustion. When I did finally stop, forced
to catch my breath, I was approached by a kind park worker. He

asked me my name, but by then the panic had such a tight grip that I could only manage the pitiful, monosyllabic responses of children and others crying in uncontrollable desperation.

"What's your name, kid? It's going to be okay. I can help you."

"I-I-I...D...Don...Don't...Kn...Kno...Know." Each syllable escaping between gasps as the panic monster chokes the words.

"Calm down, kid. Get it together. You're eighteen years old, you're embarrassing yourself!"

Ha! Just kidding. I wasn't really eighteen. I was an eight-year-old terrified kid, and I still remember that feeling of panic. Because sometimes you're lost and you know it.

I have some good news and some bad news for us as leaders. Here's the bad news first. You're going to get lost. It's just going to happen. You're leading, staying faithful, trying to do things right. You know the ultimate set of goals, and it looms ahead of you like a mountain in the distance:

Grow my church in numbers and in health.

Help my family love God and love each other.

Lead a profitable business that honors God in the way we do business.

But moving toward that mountain, you're going to pass through unfamiliar territory before you get there. There are metaphorical forests, swamps, and amusement parks between you and the goal. And at times you won't know where you are or which way to go. But the worst part of being lost is that panic will be there to greet you with a suffocating hug if you let it.

Here's the good news. Getting lost doesn't have to be a panic-filled experience. It can actually be good for you as a leader and can take you to new places. IF you can keep your head. IF you get past the panic. IF you think clearly. IF you are prepared for getting lost.

That reminds me of Rudyard Kipling's great poem "If." Listen to the first few lines:

> If you can keep your head when all about you
>   Are losing theirs and blaming it on you,
> If you can trust yourself when all men doubt you,
>   But make allowance for their doubting too;
> If you can wait and not be tired by waiting,
>   Or being lied about, don't deal in lies,
> Or being hated, don't give way to hating,
>   And yet don't look too good, nor talk too wise:

My dad used to tell me the same thing in a simplified version: "Cool heads rule the day." Getting lost is really not that bad. It's just part of the journey. Panic is what's bad.

Another "If" statement that I like is further into the poem:

> If you can meet with Triumph and Disaster
>   And treat those two imposters just the same;

Both triumph and disaster are only temporary conditions. Keep your head and handle both temporary conditions wisely. Being lost is a temporary condition too. Don't let panic keep you from thinking clearly. Easier said than done, for sure. But it can be done, especially if you prepare.

The very definition of a leader means that someone is following you. And I suppose it's assumed that you, as the leader, know where you are going and how to get there. But that's a bit too cut and dried for real life. Leadership, as practiced in the real world, is often a lot more messy. As leaders, we don't always know where we are going or how to get there.

Thomas says it for us all in John 14:5, "Lord, we don't know where you are going. How can we know the way?" (CEB). Remember the scene? Jesus has gathered the disciples together for one last huddle before he makes his way to the cross. He washes their feet, and in John 13–17 gives some of the sweetest teachings in the New Testament:

"I'm going to prepare a place for you…" (John 14:2);
"[God] will send another Companion…" (John 14:16);
"I am the vine; you are the branches" (John 15:5);
"The Father himself loves you…" (John 16:27).

And in the middle of this last teaching session, Jesus says to his best friends, "You know the way to the place I'm going" (John 14:4 CEB). And that's when our friend Thomas speaks up. This is the same Thomas who some have given the nickname "Doubting Thomas" based on some of his statements after the resurrection. Since I don't want a nickname based on my most embarrassing mistake, I call him Thomas. And I really love this guy.

Can't you just see them huddled in that room together? Maybe Jesus is being especially tender because he knows the cross is going to devastate his friends. All their hopes and dreams will be dashed to the ground, and their faith will be shaken to its core. They are about to be the most lost they've ever been in their lives. Here's how I imagine it might have happened:

Jesus: "You guys know where I'm going and how to get there."

Thomas to other disciple (in a whisper): "Psst.… What did he just say? Where's Jesus going?"

Disciple (whisper): "I don't know. Be quiet."

Thomas (whisper): "But he said we'd know how to get there. I don't know how to get there. Do you know how to get there?"

Disciple (irritated whisper): "Shhhh, just listen."

Thomas (to self): "Well, if Jesus is going somewhere, I want to go too.... I'd better ask...." (raising hand) "Excuse me, Jesus. We don't know where you are going. How can we know the way?"

Jesus: "I am the way, the truth, and the life. No one comes to the Father except through me." (cf. John 14:6)

Thomas (to self): Uhmm, okay.... I still don't get it.

Jump ahead a few chapters in John and it's happened. The world has crashed and burned for the disciples. Their best friend, the one they knew was God's Messiah, was executed on a cross. And now their hopes and their friend are both dead. They are lost. Panic, hopelessness, and despair set in. It was only three days from the crucifixion to the resurrection, but the disciples didn't understand that. They didn't understand that Jesus's death was just a temporary condition.

As a leader, as a Christ-follower, you will come to a place where your faith is shaken and you don't know what to do or where to go next. I believe.... I'm just lost.

My church is stuck, and I don't know how to get it growing again.

My kids have turned into rude strangers, and I don't know how to get through to them.

My aging parents have become like kids again, and I don't know how to handle it.

My job has run out of steam, and I don't know what to do next.

Some might ask, "Are you still a leader if you don't know how to get to the destination?"

Sure you are! Of course, it helps to have a map of where God wants your church or business or family to go, but many times we are called to lead *off the map* into new territory. And sometimes leaders just get lost.

I'd go so far to say that if you are really going to be a significant leader, getting lost is not only inevitable but actually good for you!

There are some pretty good parallel lessons to learn from literally being lost in the woods and how that relates to being lost as a leader of an organization. This advice is summarized in the acronym S.T.O.P.:

S—Stay calm: You can't use your brain well if you're in a panic. Breathe slowly and deeply. Drink some water, eat a little something.

T—Think: How did you get here? Get out your map and see what you can figure out.

O—Observe: Look for your footprints. What about landmarks? Find the clues and maybe you can solve the mystery of where you are.

P—Plan: If you're pretty sure of the way back, move carefully. Mark your trail as you move—piles of stones, broken branches. That way you can always come back to where you were.[1]

This same S.T.O.P. advice can help us as leaders when we get lost. Here's another article I found from 1946 about the same idea (with my emphasis):

---

1. "S.T.O.P." guidance is from Rich Haddaway, "Lost in the Woods! Now What?" Boys' Life, https://boyslife.org/outdoors/1200/trail-tips-lost-in-the-woods/.

A CLEAR HEAD WILL FIND ITSELF..."Finding oneself when lost is the test of a man," says a veteran of the Forest Service who has seen men, women and even children save themselves by sheer pluck and presence of mind. Loss of mental control is more serious than lack of food, water, clothing or possible proximity to wild animals. The man who keeps his head has the best chance to come through in safety....

It is better to carry a clear head on your shoulders than a big pack on your back. Yet in going alone into the forest it is well to go prepared to get lost. A fish line and a few hooks, matches in a waterproof box, a compass, a map, a little concentrated food, and a strong knife carried along may save a lot of grief....

A thinking man is never lost for long. He knows that surviving a night in the forest, he may awake to a clear dawn and readily regain his location.[2]

I love that idea—"go prepared to get lost." So what might that look like for leaders? Here are some steps for the leadership trail:

1. Anticipate getting lost from time to time as a normal part of the journey.

2. Panic is the enemy. Clear thinking is your friend.

3. Stay alive. Shelter, water, and food are essentials for physical survival. Make sure you take care of the essentials for your *spiritual survival*: scripture, prayer, fellowship, serving, etc.

4. Mentors are like guides. Books, seminars, and training are like maps.

5. Get to high ground for a better view. Take a spiritual

---

2. "What to Do When Lost in the Woods," scanned document, 1946, US Forest Service, https://www.fs.usda.gov/Internet/FSE_DOCUMENTS/stelprd b5435268.pdf.

retreat away from your "lostness." Try to get a thiry-thousand-foot perspective.

6. Keep going.

If we do these things, we can adopt the saucy attitude attributed to Tennessee frontiersman Daniel Boone: "I've never been lost. . . . just didn't know where I was for a while." In a very real sense, "lost" is an attitude. Now you can say, "Relax, everybody! We're not really lost. We're just exploring!"

Being lost as a leader is both an inevitable and temporary condition. So, what do we do when we are found? One of the sayings at Harvest Church that we've adopted from others is "Found People Find People." That saying is based on doing the Great Commission. It's carrying on the "family business." When you get found, go find somebody else who's lost! Jesus said, ". . . the Son of Man has come to seek and to save that which was lost" (Luke 19:10 NKJV). Finding lost people was Jesus's business, and he passed it along to us. There are lost people all around us. Sometimes they know they are lost and feel the panic. Stress from work, finances, and relationships make them think, "There's got to be more to life than this." They are lost and afraid. But others are lost and don't realize they're lost. They are riding through life, doing the best they can, thinking that everything is just fine.

You can be lost and know it.

You can be lost and not know it.

I've been both.

Remember the game Hide and Seek? I'm sure you've played this in one form or another. There are actually several variations to this game, and I have a favorite. Of course, there is the one person who is "IT." That's the seeker, the looker, the finder. Everyone one else is a hider. Kids scatter. IT counts. And when the countdown concludes, the declaration is shouted, "Ready or not, here I come!" Then IT begins to seek. So far, this is probably pretty basic for most Hide and Seek games. But here's the variation I like. When IT finds the first person, that person becomes IT also. Now there are two ITs seeking, looking, and finding. When the next person is found they also become an IT. Once found, your assignment is changed from hiding to help seeking. And so it goes. With each person found, a new IT seeker is born, and the game continues until the last hider is found.

Every day you meet people who are lost. Some know it and some don't.

When Jesus finds you, you inherit the family business.

Because found people find people.

Tag! You're IT.

Questions for Discussion

1. When's the last time you've been literally lost? How did you feel and how did you handle it?

2. Can you relate to the feelings of panic associated with being lost?

3. Have you ever been lost as a leader in a situation where you didn't know the next step for your church, business, or family? What did you do? What might you do differently now?

4. What do you think of Daniel Boone's tongue-in-cheek statement about never being lost? If you could adopt a similar attitude, how would it affect your life?

5. What would it look like if you "went prepared to get lost"?

6. Have you ever played Hide and Seek in the way described in this chapter? How does this compare with the Great Commission?

Chapter 8

LEADERS AND THE SUPERNATURAL

One of the chaise-horses was on a sudden so lame, that he could hardly set his foot to the ground. It being impossible to procure any human help, I knew of no remedy but prayer. Immediately the lameness was gone, and he went just as he did before. In the evening I preached at South-Brent; and the next day went on to Bristol.

—John Wesley's Journal, September 2, 1781

Neither by power, nor by strength, but by my spirit, says the LORD.

—Zechariah 4:6 (CEB)

Have I told you about my friend Ms. Kitty? She passed away a few years ago as a vibrant, tough, sweet, Southern, eighty-plus-year-old lady. Ms. Kitty (and now her family) own the land where Seri and I often ride, and I'm grateful for their generosity in allowing me to continue. When Ms. Kitty was alive, I'd often stop by her house at the entrance to the property and check in with her to let her know I was there and see if she needed any help around the house. There was sometimes a lightbulb to be changed or some firewood to be moved, and I was glad to help.

A few hours later, after our ride, I'd stop in again to give her a report of what I'd found on the property and the animals I'd seen. I also knew Ms. Kitty would have some cold ice tea and probably a little dessert waiting for me too. Though her horseback days were over, I'd see a twinkle in her eye as I related our adventures of the day. "I'm a good mind to hop on a horse and ride with you one day, Jim!" she'd say with a laugh. She knew that land like the back of her hand because it's the family farm and she grew up there as a little girl. I feel sure she rode her horse over every square inch of that land she loved.

The property is beautiful, and many of the horse stories in this book happen there. In fact, I've spent many hours riding and writing there on horseback. Seri and I will be riding along, and I'll get an idea for a new chapter or story to relate. So we'll slow to a walk, and I'll jot down some notes on my cell phone. One of the interesting things about the six hundred-plus acres is its diversity. There are trails, field roads, hardwoods, pines, creeks, and pastures to explore, and every ride is a little different. There's also a lot of wildlife, which makes it interesting most days... and a bit dicey on others.

My most recent unexpected "unsaddling" occurred when a deer jumped out in front of us on a back trail at Ms. Kitty's. The deer jumped up, Seri jumped sideways, and I fell down. As I was picking myself up off the ground, I mumbled, "Come on, Seri, it was just a deer. Don't jump like that." Fortunately, she had not run away but was standing just a few feet away, patiently waiting for me to get up. She had a bit of an innocent, embarrassed look on her face as if to say, "Sorry about that, buddy. I thought it was a ninja sasquatch so I was getting us out of there. Why didn't you hold on?"

It's usually fun seeing wildlife on horseback and I made a list of the animals I've come across at Ms. Kitty's place and on other rides. Here it is in alphabetical order: alligator*, armadillo, bear*, beaver, butterfly, buzzard*, coyote, cow, dog (wild dogs), deer*, fox, hawk, hog, opossum, owl, quail*, raccoon, snake, turkey*, turtle. The asterisk beside some of the animals indicates a dicey encounter I had with the creature, though I'm glad to say I didn't hit the ground each time.

This story involves a close encounter with the much unappreciated buzzard. Actually, not one but about 120 birds up close and more personal than I wanted to be.

I hadn't been to Ms. Kitty's place in a few weeks, so Seri and I were glad to be back. We had been riding about an hour, crossing familiar streams and looking for deer on hardwood trails. After riding a familiar circuit, I decided to check out a corner of the property that I hadn't visited in a while. It's a wild part of the land that you can hardly get to except by horseback. Later, I learned this wild area is called "the graveyard." During winter, the foliage from the trees was more thin and bare, and the grass was lower too. As I made my way through this part of the territory, I began to notice bones on the ground. As I looked closer, I found skulls too, grinning back at me, some with one jaw missing.

Now, I'm not easily spooked, or a person who jumps with every sound. But this was a little creepy—no one around for miles in wild country, and I come across all these bones. Seri wasn't crazy about it either, so we looked around long enough to prove to each other we weren't afraid, and then we headed for more familiar territory.

When I stopped at Ms. Kitty's on our way out, I described the path I took and told her about finding the bones. "Oh yes," she said. "That's the cow graveyard." She went on to explain that for years and years she and her family before her had raised cows on the land. And unfortunately, sometimes your cows die by disease or predator. I hadn't really thought about it before, but burying a cow is a monumental task that takes a lot of work. It was much easier to drag the carcass to a far-off, wild part of the land and let the carnivores do their work.

The cow graveyard

Knowing the reason for the bones dissolved any spooky feelings I had about that part of the land, and Seri and I rode back there many times with renewed interest, looking for different kinds of bones. Until that one day when I had a very weird and unusual encounter.

Months later, Seri and I had been riding for a while, and I decided to make a loop through the graveyard and see if the wind, rain, or creatures had unearthed any new bones. We were about a hundred yards away from the graveyard, winding through a twisted trail of scrub oaks when it hit us both. A putrid smell of rotting flesh. It was so strong that it stopped Seri in her tracks. The wind had shifted and now blew from the direction of the graveyard. At first, all I thought about was the smell. What could be so strong? I knew Ms. Kitty didn't keep cows anymore, so what in the world could be so big and so dead to give off that kind of choking aroma?

And then I began to think of predators. *Okay, something is dead up ahead. Bears and coyotes may be attracted by this smell.* Now, what to do? Seri was spooking a bit under me, not wanting to go on, but I was curious. We couldn't see very far ahead of us because the scrub was thick and the trail was winding. I gave Seri a reassuring pat and decided to press on. She reluctantly cooperated, fighting her instincts of "flight" triggered by the smell of death. As we wound through the scrub oak trail, I listened intently for any sounds up ahead and watched for any ambush opportunities a predator might have on us. I didn't realize the trail was so long as we wound through, turning corner after corner. Then we turned the last corner before the graveyard itself, and I was faced with something I'd never seen before.

We had approached quietly because I wanted to hear if anything was feeding. But as we turned the last corner of the trail, Seri and I came face to face with at least a hundred—if not hundreds—of buzzards just yards away. The bending trail had allowed us to come right up on this flock without being seen until we turned the last corner and were standing eyeball to eyeball. They were on the ground, and they covered the small trees, their weight even bending the trees at odd angles. In fact, they covered everything in my immediate vision.

The buzzard is a large black bird with a wingspan of about six feet. They eat carrion, which is dead meat, and have an incredible ability to eat things no other creature can. What might kill you or me is a pleasant snack for the buzzard. They aren't beautiful by any definition, but they do an important job that no one else wants. They eat dead, rotting meat.

I wasn't thinking of any of these nature facts at the moment. I knew it wasn't in their nature to attack, but I just hoped they knew it too and that none of them had ever seen Alfred Hitchcock's film *The Birds*. I was wondering how more than one hundred surprised buzzards and one Arabian horse were going to react to each other, so I got a good grip on the saddle. Slowly, almost as if with looks of disdain, the buzzards took flight in small groups, relieving the bent trees that they had been sitting on. Seri, who had been just as surprised as me and the buzzards, was taking it all in with nervous energy. I tightened up on the reins and held her still, but she pranced nervously as the birds took flight.

It was an eerie sight and sound. Hundreds of wings that big beating that close seemed to concuss the air all around me and change the air pressure. It's an experience hard to explain. And then to our left, in the graveyard itself, was the answer to our mystery. A dead horse carcass, about a week old, rotting and half eaten, was the source of the smell and buzzard banquet. There were about fifteen buzzards sitting on and beside the carcass, reluctant to leave their table, and they glared at us as we approached. Seri and I just stared back as if in a battle of wills, and they eventually took flight to join their comrades at a more comfortable distance. Always watching.

It turns out that one of Ms. Kitty's horses had died about a week earlier, and she had gotten someone to use her tractor to drag the carcass to the old cow graveyard. I wish you could have been there with Seri and me as we rounded that last corner to be greeted by the buzzards in the cow graveyard, because it was a sight that I think I'll never forget.

The cow graveyard was really creepy that day. Human cemeteries, of course, are a lot more pleasant. Many of them are quite beautiful with well-manicured grass and garden themes. There may be songbirds flitting through the trees but certainly no buzzards. With modern-day caskets and vaults in the ground, we don't expect to see a bunch of bones lying on the ground or poking out of the grass. That would be shocking.

And I suppose it was for Ezekiel too. This is a Bible story that comes to mind every time I ride through the cow graveyard and see the bones on the ground.

Here's the story from Ezekiel 37:1-3 (NLT):

> The LORD took hold of me, and I was carried away by the Spirit of the LORD to a valley filled with bones. He led me around among the bones that covered the valley floor. They were scattered everywhere across the ground and were completely dried out. Then he asked me, "Son of man, can these bones become living people again?" "O Sovereign LORD," I replied, "you alone know the answer to that."

Ezekiel is a prophet and priest at work in 571 BC. Jeremiah had warned for years that God was going to punish Israel if they did not change their hearts and turn to back to the Lord. The people refuse to listen, and the nation is conquered by Babylon in 587 BC. Many of the Jews find themselves in exile there. And Ezekiel is with them, teaching and urging the people to turn their hearts and lives to God.

Ezekiel has experienced other supernatural images while in the Lord's Spirit, so perhaps he's not as shocked as you or I would be by this event. But it still has to be a bit unsettling, right? He is transported to a valley filled with bones. It seems God gives him time to walk among the bones and see the total devastation of death and decay. There is not the smell of rotting flesh because there is no flesh. Whatever or whomever these bones came from has been dead a long time. The bones are old, dry, and dusty. I imagine there is silence in this valley of death. Perhaps the only sound to be heard is the wind occasionally blowing sand over these bleached bones. After having time to survey his new surroundings and check out this unexpected valley of bones, God breaks the silence of that place with a question: "Can these bones become living people again?" (Ezek 37:3a NLT).

Oh, so these were people. Not animals. That makes it a bit creepier. Dead people. I'm surrounded by dead people. Oh, the question. Hmmm, let me think. Now, the obvious answer, if asked by anyone else, is "No way! Of course not." You could wait here till forever, but these bones are drying up, not growing more alive. They are moving toward decay and dust. There is no hope, and no way for any kind of rejuvenation.

That would be the natural, logical answer to everyone else. But Ezekiel isn't talking to "everyone else." He's being asked a question by God. And Ezekiel's been around God for a while. This isn't his first rodeo. He's seen some stuff that would make your head spin. And so he gives an answer that we can all learn from when faced with the impossible: "Lord God, only you know" (Ezek 37:3b).

It's a good answer, isn't it? All my natural logic, all my reasoning, and all my experience tell me, of course, dead bones can't live again. But if I use that same logic, reasoning, and experience, and enter God into the equation, then I get a completely different answer.

Hmmm, if God is God, then he can certainly enter the natural and do the supernatural. God made humans from dirt, so he can certainly bring them back to life if he chooses. In fact, it's really only reasonable and logical to assume that when the Creator

God intervenes in creation, then the ordinary rules of nature may be suspended.

Even in our human games, when the referee steps in, he can call timeout or remove a player. The referee is not breaking the rules. The rules just don't apply to him in the same way they do to the participants. How much more when the Creator of the Universe steps into his creation?

Through the ministry of Jesus, the Creator steps into creation with miracles. Wind and waves obey a human? Illogical. Wind and waves obey their Creator? That makes sense.

So Ezekiel answers with the wisdom of supernatural logic. Humanly speaking, there's no way these bones can live again. It's just impossible. But, you are here, Lord, so anything can happen. I guess you are the only one with the real answer. It depends on you.

Having received an answer, God continues his dramatic illustration with new instructions:

> Then he said to me, "Speak a prophetic message to these
> bones and say, "Dry bones, listen to the word of the LORD!
> This is what the Sovereign LORD says: Look! I am going
> to put breath into you and make you live again! I will put
> flesh and muscles on you and cover you with skin. I will put
> breath into you, and you will come to life. Then you will
> know that I am the LORD." (Ezek 37:4-6 NLT)

Note that God doesn't speak to the dry bones. He tells Ezekiel to do that, and tells him exactly what to say. Why is that? I certainly don't know the full answer, but by observation we see that God chooses to use Ezekiel and works through him. If you think about it this way, God allows Ezekiel to partner with him to do something great. It's not an equal partnership by any means. What does Ezekiel bring to the table? Obedience, faith, and trust.

God certainly could have spoken the words and raised the bones to life. God didn't need Ezekiel, like he was some missing ingredient to a magical formula. But through the Bible we see God repeating this pattern. God chooses men and women as leaders, and he works with and through them. Frail, broken, marred, and human though they be.

And this is one of the mysteries of leadership. God often chooses to work through ordinary people like us. What do we bring to the table? Does God need our advice or expertise? Ha!

We bring obedience, faithfulness, trust, and love. God often works through very human leaders. He invites us into a partnership—not because God needs us but because he loves us.

I understand this more as a dad. There are some things that I can still do better than my young adult children. I can preach and teach better (though perhaps not for long!), and I have more experience in ministry. But, I love—LOVE—when my kids partner with me in doing ministry. I love to see the joy, excitement,

Seri and Jim Cowart at Harvest Church

and fulfillment in them as they experience helping others in ways they could not alone. It is truly awesome!

I felt that same feeling in starting a church. God was not only directing me to do a task, but he was also inviting me to partner with him in a project that I certainly could not do alone. Thousands of people have made first-time commitments to Jesus. Water wells and clinics have been built around the world. A translation of the New Testament is nearing completion for an unreached group of people. People are growing in their faith here and around the world through partnership with God. It is God's project. He just invited me to be a part. And it's made me hungry for more. I know full well what I bring to the table. I don't have much intelligence or insight or power to offer God. I'm just coming like an excited little kid saying, "God, I love you! I want to obey and trust you. What do you want to do next? I want to be a part if you want me to!"

At this point I hope you too are thinking, *God, I want to partner with you! What do you want me to do? I want to do something big with you too! Use me like you did Ezekiel!* In leadership and in following Jesus, *we have a part* and *God has a part.* Sometimes we are told to act. Sometimes we are told to wait. Sometimes we are told to speak and sometimes to keep quiet. I've noticed over the years that some of the trouble I get into is when I get impatient with my part and want to do God's part instead. Sounds ridiculous, I know, but you've probably done it too!

In one situation, God tells us to move. So we move and get in the habit of moving and might even think that's the key to success—just move! But then God tells us to wait. Wait? I don't wait, God, I'm a mover, remember? You told me to move last time. You can't go changing it up on me, God. Which is it? Do you want me to move or wait?

And God says, *It depends. Just stay close to me and do what I tell you.*

Remember that great leader Moses? He was a great man of God. But he had similar difficulties in following directions. For example, Moses had logistical challenges providing food and water for the people he's leading through the wilderness. And Moses discovers (the hard way) that God doesn't always handle the same problem in the same way. For instance:

> People are thirsty; God says strike rock; Moses obeys; water comes out; everything's good. (Exod 17 CEB)

> People are thirsty again; God says speak to rock; Moses strikes rock instead; God is angry because of his disobedience. (Num 20)

Why didn't Moses just follow God's instructions? I imagine that his logic went something like this:

Moses: "Well, the people are thirsty again. Remember that time God told me to hit that rock and water came out of it? That was awesome! Yep, that's how you obey God alright. People get thirsty, and it's time to hit some rocks."

God: "Speak to the rock, Moses."

Moses: "Yes, sir, that's just what I'm gonna do, hit that rock, Lord. Just like you taught me. I'm gonna hit that rock so theologically correct, that water's going to come out just like last time. Because that's what you taught me to do—you hit rocks when you need water."

But that's just not how God works. This is not a "one size fits all" world and there are no cookie-cutter solutions. And that's frustrating and confusing to some of us who just want to live by the rules. But relationships are richer and deeper than rules! And God wants a real, deep, intimate relationship with you. Deeper and richer than you have now. Always growing.

When Jen and I first married, we had a lot of household rules about everything: squeezing the toothpaste, paying bills, doing car maintenance, keeping up with household chores, and so on. But the longer we were married and the more we loved and trusted and respected each other, the rules, bit by bit, weren't needed anymore. When we look out for each other and work for the best of the other person, the relationship deepens and matures. Now we just have one rule. Or rather, I just have one rule assigned to me: "Don't put pictures of Jen on our Facebook page without her approval." Happy to say, I'm pleased to comply 100 percent of the time and actually remember to comply about 60 percent of the time. That's up a full 10 percent from last year, so I'm making progress. Ha!

Relationships are deeper and richer and more flexible than rules. And God wants a relationship with us based on love and trust rather than stagnant rules. But in order for this freedom to work, we must communicate and stay close to the one we love. Jesus is always our example! He said, "I can do nothing on my own. I judge as God tells me" (John 5:30 NLT). You can also paraphrase it this way: "I don't do anything of my own initiative, only what I see the Father do. That's what I do." Jesus, who is fully divine, stayed in such good communication and relationship with the Father that every move was directed and approved. Isn't it interesting and curious how Jesus heals people in different ways? There's no cookie-cutter mantra to heal the blind or deaf or lame. No secret incantation where the exact words have to be repeated just so. Not with Jesus! Sometimes he speaks, sometimes he touches, and sometimes he spits on the ground and makes mud! As Jesus is healing and teaching and leading, he is also listening. He's listening to the Father.

So Ezekiel speaks the words God tells him to speak and something amazing happens. "I prophesied just as I was commanded. There was a great noise as I was prophesying, then a great quaking, and the bones came together, bone by bone. When I looked, suddenly there were sinews on them. The flesh appeared, and then they were covered over with skin. But there was still no breath in them" (Ezek 37:7-8 CEB).

I'm not sure if Ezekiel was interested in anatomy, but it must have been an amazing sight to see. First, the skeletons join together with a rattling noise as they clink and clunk together, bones moving into the correct sockets. Then the layers of muscle, tissue, and skin wrap themselves in and around each individual until a complete human lies there where only dusty bones had been before. The bones and skeletons were literally getting dressed with flesh and sinew.

Sometimes miracles are accomplished in stages. Though a human army now filled the valley where the bones had lain, there was still no life. That must have been an interesting sight as well. Now it must look like hundreds of thousands or even millions of people, as far as the eye could see were lying side by side, sleeping in this valley. So God commands Ezekiel to speak again and to command the winds to breathe into the bodies. "So I spoke the message as he commanded me, and breath came into their bodies. They all came to life and stood up on their feet—a great army" (Ezek 37:10 NLT). And then God reveals the meaning of this elaborate visionary illustration.

Then he said to me, "Son of man, these bones represent the people of Israel. They are saying, 'We have become old, dry bones—all hope is gone. Our nation is finished.' Therefore, prophesy to them and say, 'This is what the Sovereign LORD says: O my people, I will open your graves of exile and cause you to rise again. Then I will bring you back to the land of Israel. When this happens, O my people, you will know that I am the LORD. I will put my Spirit in you, and you will live again and return home to your own land. They you will know that I, the LORD, have spoken, and I have done what I said. Yes, the LORD has spoken!'" (Ezek 37:11-14 NLT)

The Valley of Dry Bones is turned into Resurrection Valley! And God partners with Ezekiel to do it. It is a promise of new life from the exile. It is miraculous. It is supernatural. It goes against all human logic and experience. It is impossible. Except, it is possible, because God is there.

We have a saying around Harvest Church about this aspect of God's power. We say, "When Jesus shows up, anything can happen!" We even use it as a call-and-response during worship. Sometimes I'll say to the crowd in the middle of my sermon, "When Jesus shows up..." and they yell back, "Anything can happen!" It's pretty fun actually. You should try it. And it's true. When Jesus shows up, anything can happen.

This message about the miraculous power of God is one that all leaders would do well to reclaim. Some of my Christian brothers and sisters tend to throw out the baby [miracles] with the bathwater. You remember this phrase, right? There's some ambiguity about the origin of this idiom. Some claim it goes back to the Middle Ages when baths were not so frequent, typically every three to six months. It's said the head of the house would bathe first, followed by the spouse and then the children—all using the same water! That might explain the infrequency. Finally, the baby is bathed and could "get lost" in the now murky waters. Don't throw the good out with the bad.

Without question, in the past we've seen dramatic misuse or fabrications of supernatural healing and miracles. Martin Luther initiated the Reformation five hundred years ago in part because relics of saints were bought and sold in flea markets, based on the desperate need for magical healing powers. In the nineteenth century, traveling "snake oil" peddlers sold miracle cures from the back of wagons. In the twentieth century, flamboyant evangelistic characters on television promised healing if the viewer would send money. Jesus certainly never did that. But have we been so turned off by the misuse that we have thrown out the real thing?

When was the last time a genuine miracle of healing happened in our churches? What would we even do if Jesus showed up and did something like that? We enjoy gleaning the wisdom from biblical stories, but sometimes we explain away supernatural events as either a primitive (meaning ignorant) behavior in ancient times, or as a misunderstanding of natural processes that have a scientific explanation. We are, after all, educated, modern people living in a high-tech, self-explanatory world. I suspect God laughs at our human arrogance. Or perhaps weeps.

When Jesus returned to his hometown of Nazareth, Matthew records that the people there, the very people who had watched him grow up, were "repulsed by him and fell into sin.... He was unable to do many miracles there because of their disbelief" (Matt 13:57-58 CEB).

I wonder if this is how Jesus perceives the church today?

Wouldn't it be great if we as individuals and churches could see and experience miracles like Ezekiel saw and Jesus performed? What if our worship services took on a new dimension? They would not be dry and boring with an out-of-date lecture for a sermon. Nor would they be emotional displays of self-serving songs that chase the next set of goose bumps.

What if our church services consist of a time when we worship God from our hearts? When we hear inspired teaching from God's Word, instructing us how to live real lives in the midst of relevant challenges, anxieties, and hopes? And then in a time of prayer, God performs miracles of healing and restoring of relationships with each other and with himself. No spotlight on a superstar pastor or singer—just God working in a quiet but powerful way.

Would that be awesome, or would you be offended? "I'm sorry, Jesus, but I just don't think we're going to have time for that today. Besides, it's not in the bulletin!"

John Wesley was probably the most practical, down-to-earth, methodical Englishman you'd ever want to meet. He was educated, skilled in multiple languages, adept in the sciences and politics, and conducted himself with proper English manners. And...he was passionate about Jesus. The modern reader might find it difficult to read his journals due to his use of now archaic words and phrases, but if you work at it, you'll meet a genius, with real problems of personal relationships and doubts. He documents an intense, practical, logical, and yes, methodical faith—so methodical that his teaching colleagues at Oxford gave Wesley and his companions the derogatory nickname of "Methodists." It stuck.

But with all of Wesley's methods, education, and English manners, he held to—or perhaps rediscovered—a childlike faith. He believed and asked the Creator to step into creation and do the impossible, the supernatural. Since this is a book related to horses, I looked and found at least three separate occasions when Wesley prayed for his horse and it was healed.

> I set out for Derby; but the smith had so effectually lamed one of my horses, that many told me he would never be able to travel more. I thought, "Even this may be a matter of prayer;" and set out cheerfully. The horse, instead of growing worse and worse, went better and better; and in the afternoon (after I had preached at Leek by the way) brought me safe to Derby.[1]

1. *The Works of John Wesley: Journals,* May 23, 1783 (Nashville: Abingdon Press, 2015).

Albert Outler, one interpreter of John Wesley's writings, observed a pattern of four criteria that Wesley apparently used to make decisions and lead a faithful life: scripture, tradition, reason, and experience. Professor Outler described these sources of wisdom as a quadrilateral, a geometric shape with four sides, but not necessarily a square with four equal sides. In my view of John Wesley's teaching, this analogy does not mean that my experience or reasoning can lead me to believe something that is contrary to scripture. Yet some have taken "Wesley's Quadrilateral" and used it in a way that Wesley never would, justifying decisions or actions contrary to scripture because personal "reason and experience" say otherwise.

For Wesley, scripture was not just one among four criteria but the basis, the platform, the foundation that the other three criteria (tradition, reason, and experience) rest upon. For Wesley, scripture was primary. He called himself a "man of one book," the Bible.

As a leader, you're going to face situations that aren't in a "how to" leadership book. You're going to come to a place where *you* are not enough, because the situation you face is, quite simply, impossible. You don't have enough experience, intelligence, energy or charm to make those dry bones come to life. You can't do it. It's impossible...unless Jesus shows up. Because when Jesus shows up, anything can happen. A leader following Jesus means being a leader who listens to God. The relationship is close and intimate and growing.

Here are a few things to remember that might be helpful the next time you encounter a "valley of dry bones."

1. Remember, God has a part and you have a part. Do your part, not God's part.

2. Ask. Seek. Knock. (See Matt 7:7.) "You long for something you don't have, so you commit murder. You are jealous for something you can't get, so you struggle and fight. You don't have because you don't ask.
   You ask and don't have because you ask with evil intentions, to waste it on your own cravings."
   (Jas 4:2-3 CEB).

3. Follow instructions from God closely.

4. God doesn't seem to use cookie-cutter techniques, so follow the rules but lean into the relationship so you'll know what to do.

Maybe we'd see more supernatural events of God's power in our leadership and our churches if we just asked more. I think that's where I'm gonna start.

Questions for Discussion

1. Ezekiel found himself in the Valley of Dry Bones. Have you ever faced a challenge as a leader that felt like an impossible task?

2. When God asks Ezekiel if the bones can live again, he says, "Lord God, only you know." Why do you think Ezekiel said that? What would you have said in the past? What would you say today?

3. What do you believe about miracles and why?

4. God partners with Ezekiel to bring the bones back to life. You probably haven't faced the exact same experience, but have you ever felt God invite you to partner with him on something?

5. "In leadership and in following Jesus, we have a part and God has a part." Discuss this statement and talk about the specifics of our parts and God's parts.

6. In Numbers 20, why do you think Moses disobeyed and struck the rock instead of speaking to the rock as he was told?

7. What in your sphere of influence might be considered a valley of dry bones? A relationship, church, marriage, denomination, or someone's faith?

8. What do you think would happen if people were suddenly healed during a song in your church service?

9. Have you ever thought that God doesn't do miracles anymore? Why?

10. If God wanted to do something big but out of your comfort zone in your life or church, how would you respond? How would those around you respond? Why?

Chapter 9

WHEN LEADERS FACE REJECTION

My treasures do not ching together or glitter. They gleam in the sun and neigh in the night.

—*Bedouin Proverb*

Then the whole city came out and met Jesus.
When they saw him, they pleaded with him to leave their region.

—*Matthew 8:34 (CEB)*

I've shared often enough that Seri and I are always looking for new trails to explore. But sometimes this has led to some...uh...trouble: Namely, being asked to leave a certain place. Actually, I'm a bit embarrassed to say this has happened more than once.

I suppose this stems from some faulty assumptions on my part. Here's how I think:

"I love Seri! She's awesome. She's beautiful and I love to be around her. Just looking at her brings me peace and joy, like looking at a magnificent painting or listening to powerful music. She is a masterpiece that inspires! Just watching her stirs my soul with different emotions—sometimes calming me and sometimes stirring me up with energy and excitement. It's as if being with her makes me better. When I'm with her, somehow it seems some of her beauty and courage and power are absorbed into me, inspiring me to be a better person. And I'm sure *everyone else* must feel the same way. It's just a blessing and a privilege to be around any horse—but this horse especially!"

Did you catch the faulty part? It's still hard for me to believe that not everyone feels the same way I do about horses. After all, listen to the Lord describe the horse to Job as one of the greatest animals made by the Creator.

Noble Seri

"Have you given the horse its strength
   or clothed its neck with a flowing mane?
Did you give it the ability to leap like a locust?
   Its majestic snorting is terrifying!
It paws the earth and rejoices in its strength
   When it charges out to battle.
It laughs at fear and is unafraid.
   It does not run from the sword.
The arrows rattle against it,
   and the spear and javelin flash.
It paws the ground fiercely
   and rushes forward into battle when the ram's horn
   blows.
It snorts at the sound of the horn.
   It senses the battle in the distance.

112

It quivers at the captain's commands and the noise of battle. (Job 39:19-25 NLT)

Wow! That praise of horses makes me want to drop the mic and walk away, people! What a description of a magnificent animal created to embody courage and nobility!

We see some of this admiration in Mohammed's description of the Arabian horses as "daughters of the wind" or "drinkers of the wind." The Arabian legend of the creation of the horse reflects the honor and respect the early bedouin people had for these animals.

> I have heard that when God, praise be unto Him, desired to create the horse he summoned forth the South Wind, which the people of Egypt call El Marees saying, "I shall create from thy substance a new being which shall be good fortune unto my followers and humiliation to my enemies. Condense thyself!"
>
> And the wind condensed itself. And the angel Gabriel caught a handful of it and said to God, "Here is the handful of wind."
>
> And God created there from an Arab horse of bay color and addressed him saying, "I have created thee and named thee *faras* (horse). I have bestowed my blessings upon thee above all other beasts of burden and made thee their master. Success and happiness are bound to thy forelock; bounty reposes on your back and riches are with you wherever you may be. And I have endowed thee to fly without wings; you are for pursuit and flight. And thou shalt carry men who will glorify me, and thou shalt glorify me with them thereby."[1]

Throughout the millennia, there have been "people of the horse" who love and respect and live in companionship with this noble animal. From the Bedouin people of the Middle Eastern deserts to the Native Americans of our Western plains, people

---

1. Judith Forbis, *The Classic Arabian Horse* (New York: Liveright, 1976), 75.

have formed bonds and partnerships of love and respect with these "drinkers of the wind." But evidently not *everyone*. Which explains in part why I've been kicked out of places.

A horse and her boy

That's Not Fair

The Georgia National Fairgrounds is located in our county. The fair itself only comes to town for two weeks in October, but the campus is used year round. The facilities and grounds are beautiful and well kept, with barns, ponds, convention halls, and open fields and meadows. There's always something interesting going on there: dog shows, art shows, concerts, RV camping, and more. If you are ever passing through Perry, Georgia, you should stop by and check it out. But not if you're on horseback, and you probably shouldn't use me as a reference. Ha! Here's the story.

My family loves going to the fair, and the Georgia National Fair is a big one. Hundreds of thousands of people attend every year. There's food, concerts, rides and masses of people to watch. The hustle and bustle is exciting. But when the fair is not in town, it's quieter. One day I thought, "Hmmm, I wonder if it would be okay to take Seri out there and ride around. Think I'll try it."

On my day off, I loaded Seri on the trailer and headed out. We parked across the street from the fair-grounds, had a nice picnic under some spreading oak trees, and then saddled up. Now, I'd like to make this point clear: I did not sneak in. The

Seri and her pal Lucy

property is completely fenced in with gates and guardhouses at the main entrances. Seri and I rode up to the guardhouse at the Livestock Gate and looked in. Nobody there. Now, I suppose I did have a thought pass through my mind that I might not be completely welcomed to ride around, but I dismissed that quickly as I tend to think everyone would be honored and excited to have Seri pay an impromptu visit. Plus, I was working from the "better to ask forgiveness than permission" philosophy that day. After all, I tried to ask permission, nobody there, gate is open, so that said to me, "Come on in and make yourself comfortable." Ha. But that turned out to be a misinterpretation.

So Seri and I proceed to saunter on in. As is often the case, I saw what looked like a horse show going on in a nearby arena, so we rode over to check it out. People and horses were practicing and milling around, and I was told by some friendly cowboys that contestants were arriving throughout the day and the show started tomorrow. It was a quarter horse show.

You may not know this but some horse people tend to be a bit biased about their particular breed of choice. I suppose it's the same in other segments of life too. Some people are Ford people while others are Chevy people. Some are Mac and some are Microsoft. Now, I love all the horse breeds, and the quarter horse is a tough athlete. They are muscular, stocky, and fast. In fact, they get their name because they are sprinters and can run a quarter of a mile like nobody's business. The thoroughbred is the master of the Kentucky Derby race track, which is over a mile in length; But the Arabian excels at long distances, with some races of one hundred miles!

The cowboys and I exchanged compliments on each other's horses, and then Seri and I went off to explore different parts of the fairgrounds. Little did I know at the time that my new cowboy "buddies" weren't friends at all but tattletales. That's right, I said it. Turn in your spurs, you little tattletalers, because John Wayne would be embarrassed by you. You'll see what I mean.

Seri and I had been exploring for about twenty minutes and had meandered past ponds and pecan trees to a distant part of the campus. All of a sudden I hear angry shouts from behind and look back to see two security guards approaching at the top speed of their little golf cart.

We started walking toward them, and they pulled in front of us, and I could tell these guys were agitated and excited. They were probably just bored to tears and glad for a little excitement to spice up their day. "Intruder Alert! Go to Defcon 3. Where's my bullet?"

This seemed like a time for diplomacy so I put on my biggest smile and greeted them warmly.

> Me: "Hey, guys, how's it going? Sure is a nice day today, isn't it?"
> Them: "You're not allowed to be here!"
> Me: (with a big smile) "Oh, okay, sorry about that. I checked at the front gate, but no one was there so I just came on in."
> Them (worried looks): "No one was at the gate?" (I got the impression it was supposed to be one of them.)
> Me: "No, sir."
> Them: "Well, you can't be here if you aren't part of the horse show."
> (How'd they know I wasn't part of the horse show? Tattletale cowboys, that's how!)
> Me: "Okay, sure thing. Sorry if I caused you any trouble. We'll be glad to head out right now."

They seemed to relax a bit, and we headed back to the main gate together, them serving as my escorts. We were about a ten-minute ride from the gate, and by the time we arrived we were all laughing and talking comfortably with each other. The tension of the moment had faded away.

Now the story takes an interesting turn. When we arrived back at the main entrance, several things happened at once. My two new security buddies introduced me to a third guard, who was now coming out of the guardhouse. She was a young African-American woman with a twinkle in her eye and a friendly smile, and she seemed to be a bit higher in rank than her counterparts in the golf cart. I liked her right away. As we were being introduced, the second thing happened.

I don't know how to put this with literary gentility, so I'll just say it. Seri dropped a HUGE load of "road apples" right smack in the middle of the entrance to the fairgrounds. I mean, it was impressive! It was as if she were responding to the insult of being thrown out. And once she started, there was no stopping until there was a HUGE pile of fresh poop piled high right in the middle of the road. I thought this was hilarious!

The young lady started laughing too and said, "Well, I guess your horse is showing what she thinks of us!"

But the two security guys weren't laughing, probably because they were figuring they were going to have to clean it up. I didn't want to lose the good rapport I has gained with these guys, so quick as a flash I smiled and said in a cheerful voice, "No worries, fellows, I'll clean that up. Here hold my horse." And suddenly the security guard closest to me found himself face to face with a big Arabian war-horse that had just shown her contempt for the situation. It all happened so fast that the guard was holding Seri before he fully realized what was happening. He held the reins at arm's length, but Seri came in closer to investigate, and the guard backed up nervously. I hope you don't think less of me to know that I reveled a bit at his discomfort. I mean, who would throw Seri out?

But now I had my own quandary to confront. How to dispose of a heaping pile of fresh horse fertilizer? The solution came from an unexpected source.

The young female guard spoke up suddenly and said, "Hey, I've got some trash bags and a broom in the guardhouse. Will that work?"

"That would be great!" I said.

She brought out the gear, and I got to work. It only took a few minutes, but I wasn't even finished when the female guard spoke up again with unexpected excitement. "Hey, what are you going to do with that? Can I have it?" she asked. I started laughing and said, "Well, I don't have any plans for it. Sure you can have it. Why do you want it?"

"I want to put it in my boss's desk as a joke!" she said laughing. And then my day was made.

"Let me get this straight. You want to put this horse poop in your boss's desk as a joke—your boss, whom I assume is the head of security." It took a few seconds for this to sink in, but then I said, "I think that is awesome, but I sense it is time to make my exit!"

And so we left. Kicked out. Shown the door. Ejected. Evicted. Expelled. Ousted. Removed. Sacked. Discharged. Bounced. Run off. Because not everyone likes horses. And not everyone likes me. And not everyone is going to like you either or follow you as a leader. Rejection is something that happens in life and leadership. If leadership is helping people go to a new place, what do you do when those people don't want to go? Or, don't want to go with you?

Pork Chops and Poltergeists

Even Jesus faced times of rejection in his ministry—not only from the Pharisees and Sadducees when he broke their rules, but even by his own hometown (Luke 4:28-30) and from his siblings (John 7:5).

At least once, a whole town saw Jesus's power to heal but were so afraid or offended or something that they asked Jesus to leave. Booted. Kicked out. Shown to the door, and by the very people he was trying to help. I wonder how Jesus felt when he was asked to leave the town of the Gadarenes.

Here's the story. I'm not sure how much time passes in Matthew 8, but it is chock full of activity at a high rate of speed. A lot

119

happens in a day or two: Jesus heals a man of a skin disease, as well as healing Peter's mother-in-law and a Roman officer's servant and many others, and then calms a storm with his words. Chapter 8 begins with these words: "Now when Jesus had come down from the mountain, large crowds followed him" (Matt 8:1 CEB).

Leading Large

Let me chase a rabbit trail for a minute. As leaders, this is what most of us want right? Big crowds. If we lead, we want to lead as large and as effectively as we can. I'm sure there can be a dark side to this if ego and pride get involved, but it's not bad to desire growth. We want our organization or church or business to grow and be successful. And that's a good thing.

"A king's glory is a large population, but a dwindling people is a ruler's ruin" (Prov 14:28 CEB). That second contrast is kind of funny. A prince without subjects is not the prince of much. Leaders lead people. But if no one is following, you're not really leading. You're just going for a walk by yourself. I suppose we get in trouble when we love the "crowd" but not the actual people. Jesus loves the people. We also move toward an unhealthy place when we begin to compare ourselves and our churches to others. We're on shaky ground if we are overeager to know our colleagues' attendance, budget, and membership. "Each person should test their own work and be happy with doing a good job and not compare themselves with others. Each person will have to carry their own load" (Gal 6:4-5 CEB).

So how do we balance ambition and drive as a leader without slipping into unhealthy arenas loaded with piles of comparison and jealousy? The parable of the talents from Matthew 25 gives us some pretty good guardrails. In the parable, the man going on the journey gives to his servants differing amounts of money according to their abilities. On his return, he has equal praise for the servants who worked hard and invested what they were given, even though they made different amounts of profit. The only one who angers the master is the one who did nothing worthwhile with what he was given. In fact, he simply hid it.

So maybe you're a "seven talent" person and I'm a "three talent" person. I don't need to compete with you. I just need to be faithful with the three put under my responsibility and develop those three into as much as I can grow them.

I remember a particularly overwhelming time in the early years of our church plant. I was depressed, discouraged, and felt like I was just keeping my head above water. It was probably a Monday.

I remember praying and saying something like this to God: "Lord, I'm not sure I'm the one to do this. I don't really know what I'm doing, and I feel overwhelmed. Maybe you should send somebody like Rick Warren here. I'm sure he's a better leader than me, and he'll know what to do." And then God said back to me, softly at first, but with growing intensity."Jim, I know you feel lost, but just keep going. I'm still with you. And yes, Rick Warren is a better leader than you.... But HE'S BUSY RIGHT NOW DOING WHAT I TOLD HIM TO DO. I WANT YOU TO DO WHAT I'M TELLING YOU TO DO!"

Yipes! Yes, sir! Reporting for duty, I'm back on the job!

In Matthew 8, after all the miraculous activity, toward the end of the chapter Jesus gets in a boat and crosses the lake to the land of the Gadarenes. This is on "the other side of the tracks," so to speak. Gadara is an important Gentile town, but not the place good Jewish boys go. You can almost see the disciples getting nervous and fidgety as they get closer to the place "Momma told me not to go"!

Their fears are confirmed when two demon-possessed men run out on the beach, screaming at them. "I knew something like this was gonna happen!" But Jesus stands his ground. "Hey, Jesus, we're behind you all the way...way behind you. We'll just be back in the boat if you need us."

Jesus doesn't seem shaken in the least. He commands the demons to come out, throwing them into a herd of pigs (remember, this is a Gentile town so pork chops are on the menu). A tremendous miracle occurs. These men who had been possessed and dangerous are set free. We can imagine their gratitude as they look around with new eyes, free and clean for the first time in years. All hope was gone—until Jesus showed up! It's a sweet expression of God's tender love for people who have been exiled, cut off, booted out, and rejected.

So, what's the attitude of the crowd? They soon hear about this miracle and come down to see Jesus for themselves. But then the amazingly tragic happens. There is no ticker-tape parade. The mayor doesn't give Jesus the key to the city. They don't invite him into town for refreshments. They don't even say thank you. In one of the saddest verses of the bible, they ask him to leave. "Then the whole city came out and met Jesus. When they saw him, they pleaded with him to leave their region" (Matt 8:34 CEB).

What motivated these people to reject Jesus? Fear, pride, control, preservation of the status quo? I suppose these are some of the same reasons people reject Jesus today.

I can imagine the town leaders getting louder and louder as they tell Jesus to leave. Their voices rising in anger to cover their fear. Maybe people on the shore begin to pick up rocks to throw in case Jesus refuses. Maybe some of the children imitate their parents and elders by picking up stones too, thinking this is some kind of cruel game. Drive out the bad man. Don't let him stay. If that did happen, it must have broken Jesus's heart even more.

Here is God's Son, the Messiah, the King coming in peace with power to heal and give life. Maybe Jesus wanted to shout, "I can set you free! I can break the chains that hold you too. I can show you the way to God." But he gets in the boat and leaves. Just like they ask him to.

The Matthew 8 narrative doesn't tell us how Jesus feels here. But we get a glimpse later on when he's rejected again, this time by his own people. "Jerusalem, Jerusalem! You who kill the prophets and stone those who were sent to you. How often I wanted to gather your people together, just as a hen gathers her chicks under her wings. But you didn't want that" (Matt 23:37 CEB).

I imagine this same yearning would be present in God's plea to the church at Laodicea...and to my church and your church...and to me and you. "Look! I'm standing at the door and knocking. If any hear my voice and open the door, I will come in to be with them, and will have dinner with them, and they will have dinner with me (Rev 3:20 CEB).

If Jesus was rejected after relieving human suffering, you're going to experience rejection too. "Remember what I told you, 'Servants aren't greater than their master.' If the world harassed me, it will harass you too. If it kept my word, it will also keep yours" (John 15:20 CEB).

So as a leader, what do you do with that? What do you do when you want to lead, but the people don't want to follow you?

Here are a few possible responses when faced with rejection, based on this story from Matthew and others.

1. *Win the crowd over.* Leaders "should be kind toward all people, able to teach, patient, and should correct opponents with gentleness. Perhaps God will change their mind and give them a knowledge of the truth" (2 Tim 2:24-25 CEB). Share the vision with clarity and enthusiasm. Answer their questions. Connect the dots. Help them see a better future. Sometimes people just need good information and time to process it.

2. *Don't whine, complain or demand.* "Do everything without grumbling and arguing" (Phil 2:14 CEB). Complaining only makes you look, well, kind of pathetic. If you have to demand, cajole, manipulate, or remind people that you are the leader, you've got bigger problems than you know.

3. *Someone may need to leave.* It might be you. It might be your opposition. Remember Moses and the Israelites. They wandered in the wilderness for forty years for a purpose—so the "unbelieving" generation could die out.

4. *Cast your vision and see who wants to follow.* If no one does, it might be time to "go where the fish are biting."

5. *Deal with conflict.* "If possible, to the best of your ability, live at peace with all people" (Rom 12:18 CEB).

6. Not everyone's going to like you. There are times when you can't change that. But you can disagree without becoming disagreeable. You can resist the temptation to scandalize or demonize the people who disagree with you. As a leader, don't be surprised by pushback and rejection. These things are just part of the leader's job description.

Questions for Discussion

1. Have you ever experienced rejection? If so, how did it feel?

2. Have you ever been mocked or ostracized for your faith? If so, how did you respond then? How would you respond now?

3. Have you ever been kicked out or asked to leave somewhere? If so, how did that feel?

4. "Then the whole city came out and met Jesus. When they saw him, they pleaded with him to leave their region" (Matt 8:39). Why do you think the town did this? What might Jesus have been feeling when asked to leave

5. Compare Matthew 8:39 with Revelation 3:20. "Look! I'm standing at the door and knocking. If any hear my voice and open the door, I will come in to be with them, and will have dinner with them, and they will have dinner with me." Why do you think people today reject Jesus? What could we do to help people understand this invitation is for them?

6. Do you think "the organized church" sometimes gets in the way of the Great Commission? What can we do to improve that?

Chapter 10

DON'T LOWER YOURSELF TO THE LEVEL OF A NASTY OPPONENT

A person with a temper just can't train a horse.
If you start losing your temper,
you'll go backwards with a horse and lose months of training.

—Jamie Bissell, Quarter Horses, Inc.

Don't answer fools according to their folly,
or you will become like them yourself.
Answer fools according to their folly,
or they will deem themselves wise.

—Proverbs 26:4-5 (CEB)

T he alligator and I saw each other at the same time, which was way too late for both of us. We were only a few feet from each other, both surprised and now feeling a great urge to be somewhere else as fast as possible. The alligator was sunning himself on the side of the dirt road, and I unknowingly came barreling down on him while out riding Seri. Seri must have been daydreaming or looking off to the right because I could tell she was a split second behind us in recognizing the gravity of the situation. Man, horse, and alligator all shocked to find ourselves in such close proximity.

Some of the best scenes in movies are when the director shifts gears and goes to slow motion so the viewer doesn't miss the details of the action. Of course, this didn't happen for me literally, but it is amazing how much information the brain can process in a split second of time. Let me rewind a bit and bring you up to speed on this wild action Seri and I encountered.

It was a Friday, my typical ride day. Seri and I loaded up and headed to a destination I was excited about: my parents' house. Mom and Dad live about an hour south of us on Lake Blackshear. It's a beautiful part of the state with recreational water activities, fishing, and a lot of wildlife. I didn't grow up here, but Mom and Dad retired there a few years ago, bought a pontoon boat, and transitioned themselves into "Lake People." They love it. And we love it too. We'll load up on their little boat in all kinds of weather to explore the waterways and see the wildlife.

Besides the obvious reasons of wanting to be close to family, I'll admit that I had an ulterior motive that day. I'll just say it plainly, but please don't be offended. My momma can whip your momma in the kitchen! I know, I know, you probably like your mom's cooking and think it's really good. And I'm sure it is (bless your heart). But my momma, wow, her cooking is just hard to describe. It's awesome. And I've got to give props to Pops too. He can grill like nobody's business, bringing out just the right flavors in a burger or a steak.

So, yes, I try to be a good son and visit my mom and dad. And yes, I usually plan my visits around meal time. That's just good sense. So today I was excited. Dad was firing up the grill with some delicious, juicy burgers, and mom was whipping up some of her homemade specialties in the kitchen. We've worked out a little system for Seri too. Mom and Dad have a fence around three borders of their yard, and the backyard runs into the lake. So we just let Seri mow (and fertilize) the grass while we cook on the grill.

We made quick work of the burgers, home-cut fries, and fix-ins. After a nice visit and some much needed digestion, I was eager to head out for a ride. This is lake country with smaller ponds and lakes dotting the landscape. Not too far from Mom and Dad's place is a whole network of dirt roads that wind through pecan trees, swamps, and forest land. This was our riding destination for the day.

I was still recovering from my burger, so the first half hour we kept things at a nice walk. But after that we were ready to pick up the pace. Horses vary in their speeds, of course, but I've mentioned that Seri can run like the wind when she wants to and she has a trot that covers a lot of ground too, which brings us up to speed with our encounter with the alligator.

We were trotting along at a fast pace, between ten and fifteen miles per hour. The dirt road was sandy and winding, and we were going through a low-lying swampy area. It had been a cool morning, but now the sun was shining warmly overhead. Seri and I were covering ground pretty fast, simply enjoying the day and the sunshine. Trees grew close on both sides of the road, and the sun cast dark shadows between areas of warm light. And that's when it happened.

The alligator was sunning itself on the shoulder of the left side of the road in one of these patches of sunlight. Seri and I were riding on the left side of the road when we ran right up on this lounging gator. Now, I've tried not to exaggerate my stories, so I've replayed in my mind the estimated size of this alligator so you can have an accurate impression of what Seri and I saw. It wasn't a monster gator. American alligators can grow to over ten feet long and weigh a thousand pounds. This one was about four and half to five feet long, which was still pretty big to me and Seri. Especially one this close. Because we were moving so quickly and the road was so sandy, we were traveling fast and quiet. And that brought us right on top of a shocked and now very irritated alligator.

Let me describe the actions of each of the participants in this surprise encounter: the gator, me, and Seri.

The Gator

I suppose anyone would be shocked and annoyed if awoken from a nice nap in the sun, and this alligator was no exception. We were about eight feet away when we saw each other, and it took us a few more feet to stop, so we were even closer. The alligator was lying with its tail toward us and exploded into motion, rearing up and doubling its body to the right, looking as if it were going to bite its own tail The gator didn't, but this brought a big head with gaping mouth directly in our path. Now, if you've seen alligators in the zoo, you can watch for hours and they might not even move. This might lull one into believing that alligators are slow and lazy creatures. But I assure you that alligators living in the wild are not slow. They can run twenty miles per hour for a short, explosive burst. The typical athlete can run about ten to fifteen miles per hour. So this alligator exploded into motion that was surprisingly violent and wild. It flipped its body from side to side, trying to get its bearings, assess its personal danger, and find the water.

Me

My mind raced when I saw the alligator almost under our feet. We were moving at a pretty good pace and two more strides from Seri would put us right on top of this five-foot gator. Several scenarios raced through my mind, and none of them were pleasant.

The alligator might bite and break Seri's leg. Large alligators can bite with a pressure of 2,125 pounds per square inch. Compare that with a human bite of only 150 pounds per square inch.

Seri could hit the brakes and I go flying and land right on top of the irritated gator with the big bite.

Seri might jump sideways and I would have a hard fall.

You can see where these thoughts are going and most ended up in horrible death or dismemberment. This all happened in a split second, and it takes longer to describe than the actual experience. But one thought rose to the top. *Jim, your best bet is to stay on top of this horse. No matter what happens in the next two seconds, you had better hold on. You do not want to be on the same level with that gator.*

So I did. I gripped as tight as I could with my legs and reached for Seri's long, flowing mane. I was determined to get the best grip I could to hold on tight. I would have pulled back on the reins, but I didn't have time. Because that's when Seri saw the gator too.

Seri

I mentioned that Seri was at least a second or so behind me and the gator in spotting each other. Maybe she had enjoyed her lunch as much as I had, and was daydreaming as we trotted along, enjoying the beautiful scenery. Whatever the reason for her ease, I knew that was about to end abruptly because the alligator had just exploded into motion only yards from us. I've exposed Seri to a lot of different things in her ongoing training—loud noises, moving objects, and tight spaces. But alligators had never been on the syllabi, and I had no idea how she would react.

Thankfully, Seri hit the brakes. I came out of the saddle, sliding up her neck, holding onto her mane for dear life. Alligator lashes back and forth and then dives off the road into the water. Everyone is shaken but safe.

Whew, I'm exhausted just retelling this. To Seri's credit, she really did the best and safest thing possible. She slid to a halt and stood there.

The alligator gave a few thrashes of his tail and made his exit. Seri snorted and stomped, not appreciating being startled by this scaly creature. And me…my heart is racing and my breathing is fast. I slide back down Seri's neck into the saddle and give a nervous laugh and offer a thankful prayer. "Thank you, Lord! That could have been so bad!"

Critics Can Be Gators

I don't really want to repeat that experience with an alligator, but I don't want to waste it either. Here's the leadership lesson: When you encounter a gator, you don't want to fall to its level.

Bad things happen at "alligator level." In chapter 9, I described dealing with rejection. In this chapter, I want to talk about dealing with your critics. So you might think of these critics as your alligators.

Here's a question for you. Who's angry, disappointed, or frustrated with you right now because of your leadership? No, I haven't been reading your email. It's just a part of leadership. When you lead, you will disappoint and anger some people. It just comes with the territory. But the big question, the really important question, is not, "How do I prevent criticism?" That effort would be futile and useless if you are really going to lead. The big question is, "How am I going to respond to criticism?" I think we really only have a few logical choices:

1. Defend yourself
2. Attack back
3. Filter, process, respond, and use
4. Ignore

Your critics are like alligators. But that doesn't mean your critics are enemies or strangers, or even that they're wrong. Sometimes your alligators are your closest friends and family. And sometimes they aren't wrong at all but are spot-on in their criticism, and you need to hear it. Sometimes alligators have a lot to say that we need to hear. But, and here's what makes them alligators, they don't know how to say it well. They have some insight into the "what," the content. But they are completely lacking in the "how" department. They don't know how to convey this information well, so they turn into grunting, roaring, hissing, and complaining alligators. At least, that's how it sounds to you.

Now, that's giving your alligator critics the benefit of the doubt. But sometimes they are just what you suspected in the first place: whiny, angry people griping and snapping about you or a decision you've made, oftentimes behind your back. But for this leadership lesson, it doesn't matter. Regardless of their motives, we still have the same alligator lesson: Don't get on their level. Whether the gators are enemies taking character shots at you from the shadows, or a dear friend who thinks you are about to make a mistake but doesn't know how to tell you in a nonthreatening way, we can respond to alligators best if we are not on their same level.

But honestly, that's a bit of an advanced maneuver, isn't it? It's just plain hard to do, and most people don't take the time and energy to practice responding kindly to critics, then evaluate, and practice again. Most of us don't deal with alligator critics from a theoretical viewpoint. It's rarely a scholastic exercise. We deal with critics from a very personal place, often a place of pain and vulnerability. And sometimes, because interactions with alligators can happen so quickly, we are "sucked down" to the critics level of engagement. We don't "choose" to become defensive or aggressive (numbers one and two above) and lash back with the same level of intensity. And that's the difficulty. We don't "choose" at all. We just instinctively react...like an alligator.

But leaders need to think and practice and learn to do better. I'd like to suggest that numbers three and four are better options when dealing with alligator critics. Neither of these responses comes naturally to most of us. They must be learned and practiced. They are a choice you can make.

Filter, Process, Respond, and Use

Here are some questions to ask yourself when facing criticism:

1. Is this person trying to help me or hurt me? (Motive)

2. Are there legitimate concerns in their criticism that I may not be seeing? (Content)

3. Have my actions or decisions been misunderstood? (Knowledge)

4. Is more information needed? (People are generally *down* on what they are not *up* on.)

5. Am I just wrong and need to admit it, and adjust course?

6. How would Jesus respond to this criticism or conflict?

I felt some of you roll your eyes at me on that last question. *Way to go, Jim, you pulled out the WWJD card to make me feel guilty.* Not at all. Remember, when asking, "What would Jesus do?" we acknowledge that constructing a whip and literally thrashing a bunch of scoundrels out of the temple may be the response required of the situation. (John 2:15)

Listen and see if there is any merit in the criticism you receive. If you can, face criticism unemotionally, listen intently for things you may need to hear, and respond sincerely with a calm "Thank you for giving me your thoughts." Then you will have pulled off the advanced maneuver.

But sometimes the right thing to do, the thing that's called for, is to do nothing at all. Just ignore the criticism and stay on mission. How do we know when to do what? That takes discernment and wisdom.

David Didn't Lose His Head

King David is having the worst day of his life. He's fleeing his capital city, Jerusalem, but not because an enemy army has invaded. Even though he thought his kingdom was stable and well established, David is running for his life because his own son has led a successful revolt against him. Absalom, his own son, is trying to kill him.

Absalom was good-looking, charismatic, and hungry for power. He made it a practice to stand outside the palace and greet people when they came in to have their disputes settled. Then Absalom would say to them:

> "No doubt your claims are correct and valid, but the king won't listen to you." If only I were made a judge in the land." Absalom would continue, "then anyone with a lawsuit could come to me, and I would give them justice." Whenever anyone came near to Absalom, bowing low out of respect, he would reach his hand out, grab them, and kiss them. This is how Absalom treated every Israelite who came to the king seeking justice. This is how Absalom stole the hearts of the Israelites." (2 Sam 15:3-6 CEB)

Sneaky, but it worked. Absalom successfully stole the hearts of the people and led a revolt that sent David running for the hills. If that weren't bad enough, as David makes his escape, he's confronted with a new type of "parade."

Before he made mistakes in his household, David was not only king but also a national hero. People sang songs about his exploits in battle. He had literally been the most popular, successful man in the known world. But everything he has built is crumbling around him on this, the worst day of his life. And now, as he runs for his life from his own son, the parade of insults starts. A man named Shimei sees David trying to escape. Certainly he wouldn't have said these things while David was in power, but weak people kick others when they are down.

> He threw rocks at David and at all of King David's servants, even though the entire army and all the warriors were on either side of him. This is what Shimei said as he cursed David: "Get out of here! Get out of here! You are a murderer! You are despicable! The LORD has paid you back for all the blood of Saul's family, in whose place you rule, and the LORD has handed the kingdom over to your son Absalom. You are in this trouble because you are a murderer!" (2 Sam 16:6-8 CEB)

But David chooses not to respond. He ignores the criticism. Several things are interesting to note. One, Shimei doesn't have his facts right. David actually spared Saul's life, rather than cause bloodshed. Two, even though David is innocent of the charges related to Saul, he is guilty of having Bathsheba's husband killed in battle to try to hide his affair. So the accusation of murderer does fit. Three, Shimei attributes all that's happening to David as retribution from God. Four, unlike you and me, David actually has the legal power as king to shut his critic up permanently. With the snap of his fingers, David's men would have gladly removed Shimei's head. But David kept his head, and because of that, so did Shimei, at least during this incident.

One of David's men even asks permission to kill Shimei. These insults would not normally be tolerated, so why allow them now? But David refuses to strike back.

> Then David addressed Abishai and all his servants: "Listen! My own son, one of my very own children, wants me dead. This Benjaminite can only feel the same—only more! Leave him alone. And let him curse, because the LORD told him to.

137

Perhaps the LORD will see my distress; perhaps the LORD will repay me with good for this cursing today." So David and his men kept walking, while Shimei went along on the hillside next to him, cursing as he went, throwing rocks and dirt at him. (2 Sam 16:11-13 CEB)

When to respond and when to keep quiet. How do we know when to do which? Discernment and wisdom. The following passage from Proverbs seems curious to me at first glance; it seems to be a contradiction, or an odd contrast. But I don't think it is. "Don't answer fools according to their folly, or you will become like them yourself. Answer fools according to their folly, or they will deem themselves wise" (Prov 26:4-5 CEB). There's a time to answer and there's a time to keep quiet. Wisdom and discernment help us know when to do what.

At a Q & A session during a Saddleback Church Conference, a very successful pastor was relaying a story regarding Rick Warren giving him advice about hiring staff. "You've got to hire from within," Rick said. "Grow up people that know your culture and this will help you grow." So the pastor did all that he could to grow and train leaders from within. After about a year, this pastor's church was still growing exponentially, and he could not grow enough leaders from within to keep up with the pace. So he approached Rick again with the same dilemma of finding good staff people. This time Rick said, "You need to do a nationwide search. Find the best people and invest your money in these leaders who will train other new leaders. You need to look outside to grow your church."

A bit flustered, the pastor blurted out, "But last year you told me to hire from within. Now you're telling me to hire from the outside! Which is it?" Rick thought for a moment and then said, "You need to do both."

Shortly after Billy Graham died, I came across an interesting video of an interview he did with comedian Woody Allen. Allen is the interviewer, and Graham is his guest in a talk-show format. After several minutes of the interview, Allen invites questions from the audience, and you can tell immediately that these are not church folks. They aren't hostile, but some of their questions seem to be asked with barbs. This is not the exact transcript but how part of the conversation went from my memory:

Audience member: Mr. Graham, I understand that you are against premarital sex. Why is that?

Billy Graham: Well, it's not so much that I'm against it. What really matters is that God is against it, and he's very clear about that in the Bible. Some people think that God made rules to ruin our fun, but that's not true. God gives us rules to keep us safe; mentally, physically, and emotionally. Suppose you went to a football game, but suddenly people abandoned the rules of the game. Players ignored the whistle and began to tackle players on the bench or even fans in the stands. Without the rules, the game would turn into chaos. God has said that sex is created for a man and woman in the rules of marriage. He gave us these rules so we could be happy when we obey him.

Billy Graham's answer was direct, gentle, and kind. He never appeared flustered by the question, and he didn't water down his answer to please his audience. He found the good balance of speaking the truth with love (cf. Eph 4:15).

By doing this, Billy Graham changed the temperature in the room. What could have been considered hostile or mocking questions (from alligators) were met with firm but gentle answers that conveyed genuine concern and respect for the asker. I'm not sure if he changed anyone's mind that night, but he earned their respect. And that's a good place to begin.

By comparison, in David's story, remember how that ends. David makes a successful escape to the wilderness, and the rebellion from his son Absalom is short-lived. David is restored to power as king and lives to a ripe old age and is able to choose his successor, another son, Solomon. King David is considered to be the greatest ruler Israel ever had and is called "a man after God's own heart" (cf. Acts 13:22 KJV). He reigned for forty years, and generations later, through his family tree, the Messiah, Jesus, comes to earth.

In a way, it would be nice to end David's story there. But David was human like us. On his deathbed, he's giving Solomon some final instructions, and after all these years, he hasn't forgotten about ole Shimei cursing him on the worst day of his life.

> Now as for this Shimei, Gera's son—a Benjaminite from Bahurim—who is with you, he cursed me viciously when I went to Mahanaim. When he came down to meet me at the Jordan, I swore to him by the LORD, "Surely I won't execute you with the sword." But you don't need to excuse him. You are wise and know what to do to him. Give him a violent death." (1 Kgs 2:8-9 CEB)

That deathbed instruction sounds like something from the Godfather movies. *I made a promise not to kill that scoundrel, but you didn't. Handle it, boy.* Yikes, don't mess with David! I'm actually glad the scriptures let us in on this bit of information. If God used rascals and even murderers in the past, I guess God can use people like me and you.

Alligator Critics are sure to enter your life from time to time if you aspire to be a leader doing something significant. That's just a natural part of being a leader. But don't get on the alligator's level. Don't become like an alligator. That won't be good for anyone.

Questions for Discussion

1. Have you ever been criticized for something when you thought the criticism was unfounded? How did you respond?

2. David was the greatest of Israel's kings, and he faced criticism, some deserved. And of course even Jesus faced massive amounts of criticism and rejection. So we are in good company! Criticism isn't something to be avoided at all costs but something to be taken, looked over, and prayed about—sometimes thrown out and sometimes acted upon. Can you think of a time when, like David, you took the criticism that was leveled at you and ignored it for lack of merit?

3. Is it hard for you to leave someone's questions unanswered or their jeers without rebuttal?

4. Do you have a hard time standing by your decisions if they are questioned?

5. Do you think being criticized is just a part of being a leader? Why?

6. Four logical choices are typically available when we are criticized: Defend yourself. Attack back. Filter, process, respond, and use. Ignore. Which ones have you chosen? Was it by choice or was it an emotional reaction? Can you think of other possible responses to criticism beside these four?

7. Why do you think David refused to respond to the insults and criticism from Shimei?

8. In Christian thought, Jesus fulfilled the prophecy of Isaiah 53:7: "He was oppressed and tormented, but didn't open his mouth. Like a lamb being brought to slaughter, like a ewe silent before her shearers, he didn't open his mouth" (Isa 53:7 CEB). Why do you think Jesus was silent in the face of his accusers (Matt 26:63)? What can we learn from his example?

Chapter 11

HEROES

John Wesley rode far enough on horseback to circle the earth 10 times.

—www.umcom.com, "10 fascinating facts about John Wesley and
United Methodism"

So then let's also run the race that is laid out in front of us, since we
have such a great cloud of witnesses surrounding us. Let's throw off any
extra baggage, get rid of the sin that trips us up, and fix our eyes on
Jesus, faith's pioneer and perfecter.

—Hebrews 12:1-2 (CEB)

I'm a preacher. I usually speak three times on a regular Sunday and spend hours each week doing research and preparation. I also practice my sermons, often on horseback. It's not unusual for me to preach my message on a back trail before Sunday morning arrives, with no one to hear but Seri. She doesn't give much feedback, but she's a good listener. With the invention of the smart phone, I can ride and make notes for adjustment at the same time.

But this practice isn't really new. My spiritual ancestors did the same thing on horseback several hundred years ago. John Wesley (1703–1791), the founder of the Methodist movement, is said to have ridden 250,000 miles by horseback in England and America.

As he travelled from village to village, I can imagine Wesley practicing his next sermon on the trail with his horse listening too.

Francis Asbury (1745–1816) has been called the "Prophet of the Long Road" because of the miles he rode to share the gospel in America. Some have estimated his travel by horseback at 130,000 miles, while others say he passed his mentor, John Wesley, with 300,000 miles.

In 1771, Wesley asked for volunteers to help the Methodist movement in the American colonies. Asbury volunteered and was chosen for that work. He landed in Philidelphia later

Our Asbury statue pose

that year and started adding on the miles. He joined a rank of horsemen that though not as famous, did more for our country than the Pony Express. They were called Circuit Riders. They rode a circuit between churches and towns to preach and teach to the settlers and pioneers.

Peter Cartwright (1785–1872) described the life of these preachers on horseback.

> A Methodist preacher, when he felt that God had called him to preach, instead of hunting up a college or Biblical Institute, hunted up a hardy pony, and some traveling apparatus, and with his library always at hand, namely, a Bible, Hymn book, and Discipline, he started, and with a text that never wore out or grew stale, he cried, "Behold the Lamb of God, that taketh away the sin of the world." In this way he went through storms of wind, hail, snow, and rain; climbed hills and mountains, tra-

versed valleys, and plunged through swamps, swollen streams, lay out all night, wet, weary, and hungry, held his horse by the bridle at night, or tied him to a limb, slept with his saddle blanket for a bed, his saddle-bags for a pillow. Often he slept in dirty cabins, ate roasting ears for bread, drank butter-milk for coffee; took deer or bear meat, or wild turkey for breakfast, dinner, and supper. This was old fashioned preacher fare and fortune."[1]

The reputation for toughness and tenacity among these Circuit Riders spread so far that a saying developed for extremely bad weather. "Nothing but crows and Methodist preachers out today!"

John Wesley exclaimed that the world was his parish. By this he meant that it was his calling to tell everyone on the planet about the saving grace of Jesus Christ. Francis Asbury's Circuit Riders took this philosophy to heart as well. One young rider reportedly asked how and where to begin his ministry. He was instructed: "Get your pony shod. Then start out northward... until you meet a Methodist coming this way... thence westward and eastward until you meet other Methodist preachers coming this way. All this will be your work." Upon receiving this answer the young man responded with a humorous understatement. "I saw at once that I had a big field."

On October 15, 1924, in Washington, DC, President Calvin Coolidge unveiled and dedicated a statue of Francis Asbury on horseback. Several inscriptions around the base of the statue remind us of the contribution from this preacher.

On the left is inscribed, "His continuious journey through cities, villages and settlements from 1771 to 1816 greatly promoted patriotism, education, morality."

1. *Autobiography of Peter Cartwright* (Nashville: Abingdon Press, 1956). www.gcah.org/history/circuit riders.

On the right is inscribed, "If you seek for the results of his labor you will find them in our Christian civilization."

On the back is written, "The Prophet of the long road."

Here's a sample from President Coolidge's speech that day.

> Our government rests upon religion. It is from that source that we derive our reverence for truth and justice, for equality and liberty, and for the rights of mankind....It is of great significance that the generation which fought the American Revolution had seen a very extensive religious revival. They had heard the preaching of Jonathan Edwards. They had seen the great revival meetings that were inspired also by the preaching of Whitfield.
>
> Francis Asbury came to America to preach religion....He did not come for political motives....His problem during the Revolutionary War was that of continuing to perform his duties without undertaking to interfere in civil or military affairs....When several of his associates left for England in 1775, he decided to stay. "I can by no means agree to leave such a field for the gathering of souls to Christ as we have in America."
>
> A great lesson has been taught to us by his holy life....The government of a country never gets ahead of the religion of a country...this prophet of the wilderness! Who can say where his influence...shall end? It is more than probable that Nancy Hanks, the mother of Lincoln, had heard him in her youth. Adams and Jefferson must have known him, and Jackson must have seen in him a flaming spirit as unconquerable as his own....He is entitled to rank as one of the builders of our nation."[2]

In Hebrews 11 we see what's been called the "Hall of Faith"— the heroes of the past that stood and fought and often died for their faith in God. These heroes are men and women who paved the way for me and you to follow. Then, in Hebrews 12:1 we read, "We have such a great cloud of witnesses surrounding us." We really are supported by these witnesses. Sometimes we feel alone as

---

2. President Calvin Coolidge Address at the Unveiling of the Equestrian Statue of Bishop Francis Asbury, Washington, DC. 1924. www.presidency.ucsb.

leaders. Sometimes lost. Sometimes we are just tired and worn out by the journey. Don't give up. Rest, take some time off. But saddle up again and get to leading. A crowd of people ahead of you are cheering words of encouragement to help you carry on. They have finished the race and want you to finish well too. And, there is a crowd of people behind you, some yet to be born, who need to follow the path you pave.

President Coolidge ends his speech honoring Asbury:

> On the foundation of religious civilization he sought to build, our country has enjoyed greater blessings of liberty and prosperity than was ever before the lot of man. These cannot continue if we neglect the work which he did. We cannot depend on government to do the work of religion. We cannot escape personal responsibility for our own conduct. We cannot regard those as wise or safe counselors in public affairs who deny these principles and seek to support the theory that society can succeed when the individual fails. America continues its own way unchallenged and unafraid. Above all attacks and vicissitudes it has arisen calm and triumphant; not perfect, but marching on guided in its great decision by the same spirit which guided Francis Asbury."[3]

Hats off and thanks to our heroes in the faith.

---

3. Ibid.

I hope you've enjoyed this book about leadership lessons learned from working with horses. But more than that, I hope it's encouraged you to move closer to Jesus, and offered some ideas that the Holy Spirit may use to make us better leaders in the mission field.

For more information:
Want to see videos of Jim and Seri in action?
    Visit www.jimcowart.org.
Jim Cowart and Harvest: www.harvestchurch4u.org
Seri and Egyptian Arabian Horses: www.pyramidsociety.org

ALSO
AVAILABLE

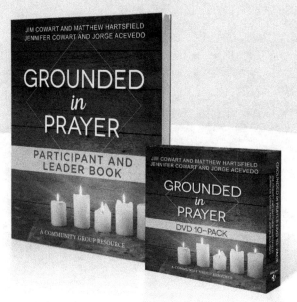

Grounded in Prayer
Participant and Leader Book
ISBN: 978-1-5018-4904-6

Grounded in Prayer: DVD
ISBN: 978-1-5018-4905-3

DON'T STOP NOW!

Keep digging into God's word. These studies are
available from Jim and Jennifer Cowart,
published by Abingdon Press.

Living the Five:
Participant and Leader Book
ISBN: 978-1-5018-2509-5

Living the Five: DVD
ISBN: 978-1-5018-2511-8

ALSO
AVAILABLE

Hand Me Downs
Participant and Leader Book
ISBN: 978-1-5018-2517-0
Hand Me Downs: DVD
ISBN: 978-1-5018-2519-4

CPSIA information can be obtained
at www.ICGtesting.com
Printed in the USA
LVHW01s2051310718
585421LV00002B/2/P